Finding the Right Fit™
The Ultimate Guide to College

Kenneth Albert

Finding the Right Fit™
The Ultimate Guide to College

Kenneth Albert

Mill City Press, Inc.
212 3ʳᵈ Avenue North, Suite 290
Minneapolis, MN 55401
612.455.2294
www.millcitypublishing.com

ISBN - 978-1-936107-02-5
ISBN - 1-936107-02-3
LCCN - 2009906236

Printed in the United States of America

Acknowledgments

I often joke with my wife that I've never had an original thought in my life and this book is no exception. My one great talent in life is that I've always been able to improve upon other people's good hard work. The Right Fit™ Program does exactly that. All of the techniques and strategies that you will find here are the culmination of both my experience and the knowledge of several fellow college counselors around the country.

I would like to give special thanks to Chuck Moore, a college consultant in Louisville, Kentucky. Chuck has been my "go to guy" for his knowledge of tax strategies and information about college loans. Chuck also has more experience than anybody I know when it comes to marketing student athletes. I would also like to give thanks to Rick Darvis, CPA, who is the founder of the National Institute of Certified College Planners, of which I am a member. Rick is probably the smartest CPA in the United States today on the tax aspects of college, especially for business owners. Finally, I would like to thank Ron Them, author of Tuition Rx program for college advisors, who has provided me with several cash flow and funding strategies.

Table of Contents

Introduction

The one aspect of the Right Fit™ Program that I do believe is unique is the emphasis on professionally administered, meaningful career counseling as the cornerstone of college planning. My research could not find any other program that truly embraces the importance of the career planning aspect of college and does so with hands-on guidance from a certified counselor. I have found that most college advice is split between two camps. The first camp focuses on funding college primarily through some type of financial planning or financial aid technique. The second camp focuses on the college admissions process and how to get into the "best" schools. What's different about the Right Fit™ Program is its emphasis on career counseling as the first and foremost priority, and the knowledge that all good things flow from there.

My deepest motivation for writing this book and for developing the Right Fit™ Program has been my frustration at the kind of college advice I see, hear, and read about every day. Although most of what I read and hear is technically correct, it always misses the bigger picture of the college process, which to me is about a person clearly understanding fundamental aspects of their personality and the motivations that drive them. It's about mentoring and guiding a teenager to clearly see those core personality traits and then apply that vision towards a meaningful college experience and subsequent career. It really doesn't matter if you save $20,000 on the cost of college only to have your child find out 5, 10 or 15 years in the future that they're in the wrong career. Is saving a little bit of money worth being miserable in the long term? Trust me when I say, that's no bargain. The most promising colleges and careers are the ones that are a good fit for a person's innate, fundamental personality traits and talents. The reality is, it's all about finding the Right Fit™.

Reader Beware

I have read thousands of books, articles, and research papers on the subject of college and I have found it a challenge to find truly good information. My conclusion is: it simply comes down to the author. Most of the written material is produced by professional writers and researchers. So, what you end up with is well written and well researched information, but it lacks the powerful insights that only real world experience can provide. I review on average two to three pieces of college literature every day, and find that even the best material will not be significantly helpful to most of those who will read it. A professional college writer is not the same thing as a professional college counselor, but it is easy to confuse the two. A good writer will do good research and report those findings. Because every family situation is different, how can the author know which strategies will help *you*? Obviously, they cannot know, and thus the writer is forced to compromise by either writing weak generic solutions or a laundry list of everything under the sun, most of which will not really benefit you. Research is not advice.

There are very few books written by experienced college counselors because we are simply too busy counseling. This book is based on my experience and the experience of my team. While some of the techniques will not apply to you, all of the information in this book goes beyond statistics and will provide you with a foundation of applied knowledge on the topic of understanding the complexities of attending college. Furthermore, you may be surprised to know that books on college are, by and large, not profitable endeavors. So, to get a real counselor to write is like pulling teeth, and I can say, with certainty, that has been my dilemma. At some point I became overwhelmed with the watered down, recycled guidance being provided and decided to just make the time to provide a real guide for parents and their students on their journey and struggle through the college process. As mentioned before, there are two basic camps in the college advisor world. The "how to pay for college" crowd focuses on the fear and angst that many families have concerning the high cost of college. In reality, this is financial planning advice disguised as college planning and I believe you should verify the person's credentials for providing financial planning advice as it relates to both college and your family's financial structure. Often, this crowd neglects the real heart of planning for college – getting the right fit to begin with. In other words, having the money to buy the wrong education is really no help at all.

The second group of advisors focuses on just the admissions part of the college process and thinks about "how to get into the best college" or "how to get into your first choice college" while largely ignoring the costs associated with it. In most cases, if your only goal is to guarantee admission, you will be forced to disregard cost as a priority. If your family cannot pay outright for college, this plan will have you taking on large sums of debt. I know several busy college advisors that charge families between $20,000 and $40,000 to guarantee admission to Ivy League schools. Obviously this excludes many families from getting their help. However, the fear of getting into a good college may be somewhat misplaced. According to The Chronicle of Higher Education (January 30,

2009), 77.8% of students were accepted to their first choice college. Further, 86.8% of students surveyed were attending either their first or second choice college. These statistics are based on survey responses of more than 240,000 first-year students entering 340 colleges and universities in the fall of 2008.

What this data doesn't account for is whether or not these kids made the right choice to begin with. It's important to understand most students got *in* just fine; however, getting *out* on time and with the right degree is another matter. As you will learn in this book, the "best" college actually doesn't exist. There does exist, however, the right fit college for your student. Often there are multiple colleges that meet this criteria and this book will show you how to find them.

Close, But No Cigar

I recently read an excellent book on college, written by a professional writer and reporter. The author did solid research and spoke to several quality college advisors across the country and was able to capture many of the finer points of college planning. Unfortunately for those readers, the author missed the most critical point of all: how to find the "right fit" for a student. Despite some excellent research, the author missed this because of a lack of experience. One experience of the author finding a college for their child does not necessarily make them an expert. If a doctor told you that they had performed one very successful surgery, would you want to be patient number two? The bottom line is that nothing can replace experience, no matter how well thought out your plan is or how much research you've done.

This book is based on experience. It explains the college crisis and how to fix it by using a tried and true program: The Right Fit™ Program. The program is based on experience gathered from 60 years of research and provides *real* career and college planning for college bound students. This book is designed for you to do as much as you like on your own. But like most things in life, the guidance of a professional is going to produce a better result. If you get stuck on something or just want to know if you're headed in the right direction, drop us an email through our website and explain that you have read the book. I can be reached at ken@kennethalbert.com.

Chapter One:
"the heart of the matter"

College Report Card

If your child was headed down the wrong path, when would you want to know? You're going to spend between $80,000 and $200,000 for one child to attend four years of college, and that's the good news. Every day, teenagers pick the wrong majors, the wrong colleges, and most importantly, the wrong careers. If you believe that it takes four years to earn a Bachelor's degree, then the following facts will disturb you. The National Center for Education Statistics provides analysis and reports directly to the US Department of Education and is the primary federal entity for collecting, analyzing and reporting data relating to education in the United States and other nations.

In May of 2005, the National Center for Education Statistics conducted a very detailed research study which produced a report called *The Road Less Traveled?* What makes it truly fascinating is the fact that the report simultaneously analyzed two separate and distinct sets of data. Furthermore, the data is based on student surveys as opposed to college-reported data. The first data set tracks students over the six-year period from 1995 to 2001 and the second data set looks at only those students who received their bachelor's degree in 2000 regardless of when they began college. Some interesting results appear on page 27 of the report: for the students who began at a four year institution with the goal of earning a bachelor's degree, only 36.5% had done so within four years. Additionally, 26.1% took more than four years, 25.5% were no longer enrolled in college and 11.9% were still enrolled six years later. <u>In sum, 2 out of 3 students fail to graduate within 4 years.</u> Why is this happening?

Of the students who ultimately earned their bachelor's degree in 2000, almost 60% attended more than one institution during their undergraduate career. The breakdown looked like this: 35% attended two institutions, 16% attended three institutions, and 8% attended four or more institutions! About 50% of the students surveyed six years after entering college, and who started at four year colleges with the goal of earning a bachelor's degree transferred to a different college in order to obtain their degree. Conversely, 72% of students who had *never transferred* were able to earn their *master's* degree within six years. Sadly, analysis of both sets of independent data shows that approximately 20% of students who enter postsecondary education dropout.

The study did not show the economic impact of delayed graduation, transferring, or failing to complete college, but a quick calculation might look like this: an extra 1.5 years of college costs ($20,000 per year) = $30,000; 1.5 years of lost wages at a starting salary of $30,000 per year = $45,000; add those together and you have an additional cost of $75,000! Remember, most scholarships are good for 4 years or less. What you need to know as a parent is that the odds your child receives a bachelor's degree in four years are slim unless you have a solid college plan. You will learn in this book that by using the Right Fit™ Program, you will increase those odds significantly.

If you ask colleges about these statistics, they blame the students. If you ask the students, they blame the colleges. According to the industry trade journal Inside Higher Education (October 22, 2008), the University of Alaska at Anchorage has suggested that success for students be measured over 10 years! They go on to suggest that a student "who enrolls with the goal of transferring and does transfer is also helped and should be considered a success." The fact is: transferring is never a good goal. At best, it's a compromise.

According to the US government, graduation rates are measured by the proportion of students who earned a bachelor's degree within six years and an associate's degree within three years. But when I ask parents and students how many years it takes to earn a bachelor's degree, the answer is four years. Clearly, there is a tremendous disconnection between what families believe colleges should do and what colleges believe is acceptable. Think about it. Colleges really only produce one thing: a degree. Isn't it also true that with few exceptions, a degree can and should be earned within four years?

How did we get here? Many believe that a lack of accountability is a major reason for this disparity. I couldn't agree more. From my vantage point, I can see no independent third-party audit function for college outcomes. In fact, in a 2009 statement from the Association of American Colleges and Universities, *Our Students' Best Work: a Framework for Accountability Worthy of Our Mission*, they indicated that basically nothing of significance had changed since the subject of accountability had first been broached in a 2004 statement. What does this mean for us as parents? Since the beginning, colleges have been left to self assess whether or not they're actually doing a good job. In the meantime, they've allowed tuition to skyrocket and student debt to balloon, all while continuing to be subsidized with taxpayer dollars.

The present debate seems to be whether or not there should be some nationally standardized testing for college graduates with the goal of determining what they've learned. Colleges and universities are objecting on the grounds that it is simply too complicated to accurately and fairly test. I agree. But that's not the major issue. The issue is that colleges should be held accountable for a few definable outcomes, such as time-to-degree completion and transfer rates. Why are kids taking 6 years to get a bachelor's degree and why are they transferring in such large numbers? Shouldn't colleges be held accountable for the type of experience your student will receive? For example why, even at many "top rated" universities, will your child be receiving instruction from a teaching assistant, as opposed to a full professor, while attending a lecture hall with 300 or 400 other students? Unfortunately, this has become an acceptable practice. That type of teaching can be done just as effectively via on-line courses at a fraction of the cost. In fact, many institutions have figured that out and are increasing their on-line content for undergraduates.

There are several efforts currently ongoing to help colleges improve student outcomes, however, most of the research and data is kept secret and only shared with the colleges themselves. That's a technique guaranteed to keep parents and students in the dark and promises to make any meaningful improvements slow to materialize. One outspoken critic has been Charles Miller, who headed the Spellings Commission on Higher Education. He has argued for more accountability from colleges and universities by stating that measurements can be made of student learning. This book will look beyond the U.S. News & World Report rankings and give you powerful and simple ways to evaluate which institutions are the *best fit* for your student. It's fascinating to see the resistance colleges have to quantifiable measures of success. Why would they want to show anybody their dirty laundry? They've gone years without having to be accountable to anyone. It seems to me that there's a tremendous irony when colleges use multiple standards to evaluate our children including the SAT, the ACT and AP exams, but when we ask colleges to submit to standardized evaluations of their performance, they object.

For the consumers, students and parents, much of what colleges choose to improve or choose not to improve will be out of our control, whether we like it or not. Colleges are simply moving at their own pace to improve student outcomes. Congress may push the process along slightly or possibly a grassroots revolt will get colleges to jump off the dime and seriously address student outcomes. In the meantime, what I want to focus on in this book are those things that <u>are</u> in our control.

Finding the Right Career

In order to better understand why students take longer than they should to graduate and why the transfer rate between institutions is so high, we will take a look at life after college. Research shows that most people today are changing careers three to seven times. Typically, this trend starts in college where students are likely to change their majors two or three times. Despite the fact that we may sample several majors in college, we still end up changing our careers later on. Why?

We have a college problem in great part because we have a career problem. A 2003 Gallup poll reported that approximately 17% of the American workforce changes jobs every year. That means that more than 20 million people are confronted with the question "What work is right for me?" 74% of these jobseekers between the ages of 26 and 40 indicated that if they could go back and do it over again, they would have obtained more and better information <u>before</u> choosing their career. In America, changing careers is the norm. Culturally, we have the mindset that we can figure these things out on our own, but in this case our fierce independence is costing us dearly. How many people do you know who have received professional career counseling advice? The fact is, many people are unhappy with their careers and the result is that most people change careers three to seven times.

There is an extensive and overwhelming body of evidence that clearly shows career counseling is of tremendous benefit. A 2003 research report published by America's Career Resource Network Association (ACRNA) titled *The Educational, Social, and Economic Value of Informed and Considered Career Decisions*, is an excellent compilation of that research to date. Despite this evidence, a survey of high school guidance offerings show that high schools were offering fewer career guidance programs in 2002 than they were in 1984. This means that the burden is now squarely on the shoulders of parents and students. It's important to note that this study also found that career counseling conducted by counselors had a substantially stronger effect than unmediated career interventions. As the father of two teenage daughters (and one pre-teen) I think I understand why this is true. Both of my oldest two children are well behaved and motivated students, but even in our close knit family, communication is often less than perfect. The more time your student spends with a professional career counselor the better off they'll be. That is why both of my daughters are receiving their career counseling from one of our other certified counselors, not me.

The US Department of Education conducted a series of studies in Missouri and Utah which produced strong evidence that secondary school development programs were of great benefit. For example, students who participated in these programs scored higher on ACT exams, enrolled in more advanced placement classes, and applied for and received more scholarships. Between 1986 and 1998 the state of Indiana both funded and conducted their own career planning program. During these 12 years they saw a 61% increase in students who applied to college. In turn, this improved their states' national ranking from 40th to 17th, clearly a huge improvement. A 2002 Florida State University study found that a relatively small investment of time can yield massive results. They found that females who took a well-designed career course graduated college on average in 50 months, compared to the 61 months for nonparticipants. This can easily amount to cost savings of between $40,000 and $60,000. Here's how: one extra year of college equals $20,000 plus one lost year of employment at $20,000-$40,000.

To quote the 2003 ACRNA study, "informed and considered career decisions are linked to improved educational achievement, attainment and efficiency. Students who make informed and considered career decisions are more likely to graduate from high school and to succeed in postsecondary education." One of the most fascinating aspects of this research showed that career counseling and planning is most effective when a career professional is involved and the counseling begins *prior* to high school. Unfortunately for most Americans, if you do participate in career counseling at all, it's either after or possibly during college. For those who do seek help, it may only be after a divorce, a job lay-off, or a self-imposed career change. Although it's never too late for mom and dad, we can and should do better for our children. Later in this book I will introduce you to The Right Fit™ Program, where career counseling is an integral and natural part of the college planning process. In fact, the first three steps of this program are focused on career counseling, designed and modified specifically for high school students. Following the first three steps of the Right Fit™ Program means making informed and considered career decisions. It represents a match between a person and a career in which the individual's natural skills, interests, values and personality type align with the individual's well-being and life goals.

Who Am I, Anyway?

As teenagers about to enter college, we make a monumental decision that will set in motion a series of events, and it is a decision we can make only once. We make this crucial decision at a time in our lives when we are least equipped to do so. Most teenagers are conflicted between what they feel they are good at, what they *think* they want to be and what they are told they *should* do. The truth is, none of these is a good reason for selecting a career and the proof is in the pudding. In May of 2008, a Gallop Poll survey of people who make $100,000 or more, found that 1 in 3 spent at least one hour per day searching for a new job! The reality is that when we are young, we do not have the life experiences necessary to make these crucial decisions. We are susceptible to poor advice and are idealistic in a manner which places us in disregard of future consequences. According to the US Department of Labor, people between the ages of 18 and 38 change jobs 10 times. The solution is simple. We need to take a new approach to college.

Most families tend to approach the college process backwards. It is typical for parents or guidance counselors to begin by asking the student these questions:

1. What are you interested in studying?
2. Where do you want to go to college?
3. What do you want to be?
4. What are you good at?

A better place to start is to ask your student why they want to go to college in the first place. You'll probably hear answers like "I want a good job", "I want to make money, "I like learning", "I want to make a difference in the world", "It's what I'm supposed to do because I'm smart", or "I don't know." How can a teenager possibly know what any of these answers really mean? They can't.

They simply don't have the life experience necessary to grasp the full meaning of what they are saying. As parents we understand this. The problem is, as parents, we generally don't know what to do about it. Even if we did, teenagers don't like taking advice from anybody, especially their parents! As a professional college counselor, one of the most interesting situations occurs when a student tells me that they're absolutely certain that they do not want the same career as their parents. At first glance you might think that this is just teenage angst. However, it has been my experience that when a teenager says they are not interested in doing what mom or dad does every day, it is because they know their parents are unhappy with their careers. As you might guess, these students are highly motivated to participate in career counseling now. Even when parents have a close relationship with their teenager, communications can be strained. Paradoxically, it is also true that your teenager is listening to you, even when you think they are not. Despite what your teenager says to your face or does behind your back, deep down they love you and care about what you think.

The only thing more dangerous than a teenager that doesn't listen to their parents is one who is overly influenced by their parents. In our experience, this occurs slightly more often when mom or dad is a professional. For example, a teenager may believe that being a doctor is the best thing to do because mom is a doctor. Why? It's common sense really. This young person sees that dad loves mom, mom loves dad, and they have a great lifestyle. So being a doctor equals love and money. I'm sure that you are aware that physicians are among the most prestigious and highest paid occupations. However, according to the *Journal of the American Medical Association* (Landon, 2003), approximately one out of five doctors report being somewhat or very dissatisfied with their careers. Now think about the enormous time and financial commitment that it takes to become a physician and it is clear that we can do a better job of mentoring our kids. Have you ever met someone who makes a lot of money but is miserable? I believe one of the worst things that can happen to a person is to be in the wrong career and make a lot of money doing it. Why? Because most of us have a strong aversion to lowering our standard of living, even if it means being happier. On the other hand, if you are poor and hate your career, you're in great shape because it is much easier to make a change.

So, ask yourself now, "What do you want a college degree to do for your child?" Do you want them to get a good job, make good money, be a productive person, or maybe just be self-sufficient so they don't move back in with you? How about "be happy?" The reality of the college process is that it is an extremely emotional issue. It's an emotional decision for both parents and students. The first place to start is to take control of the emotional aspect and get a crystal clear picture of everybody's goals. The tool you need to accomplish this objective is career counseling based on the fundamental personality traits that drive all human beings.

Hype or Type

Your first step to getting college right is to recognize hype when you hear it. Forget about trying to find the "best" college. There is no credible evidence that any particular college will guarantee personal or professional success. If this were the case, then choosing an Ivy League or a top 25 school should give those students a clear advantage over other graduates in the workforce. A survey by Forbes magazine revealed that among Fortune 300 corporations' CEOs, 87% did not attend a top 25 school for their undergraduate studies. Many parents and students get hung up on brand names and the only thing they really get in return is a very large bill and all too often very large debt. The average law school graduate begins their career with over $100,000 of debt. This is very disturbing, and I can't help but wonder if this isn't one of the reasons why our society has become so litigious. But it's not only attorneys who are affected. According to the Project on Student Debt, the proportion of students graduating with $40,000 or more in loans has increased six fold since 1993.

There is no research that shows an Ivy League college degree, or any particular college degree for that matter, provides more earning potential over a lifetime. Additionally, there is no evidence suggesting that such a degree provides more happiness, more insight, or more knowledge than any other school in the country. In fact, the only legitimate data we have comes from a 2000 federal government census study that indicated that the average college graduate can expect to earn about $1 million more than a high school graduate over a working lifetime. Their figures show that a college graduate earns on average $57,500 per year while on average a high school graduate earns $31,600 per year. The difference equals $25,900, which is then multiplied by forty years and works out to be the often quoted $1 million. So the real difference is between high school graduates versus college graduates, not between college graduates versus college graduates. The simple truth is that successful people become successful not because of the college they attended, but rather because of who they are as a person. Said another way, the college does not make the person, the person makes the college.

You can also forget about trying to select "best careers for 2010 and beyond." This kind of hype is sold to millions of Americans every year because it sells well. What it doesn't do is help people to make sound career decisions. The only thing that will really matter in the end is finding a career that is a great fit for who you are as a person. Finding out your true personality type and matching that with potential careers should be your ultimate goal.

Conventional Career Counseling

We have always understood that certain people are better at certain tasks. The conventional approach to finding a career is to determine a person's abilities and interests and then match those with a career. The problem with this approach is that it doesn't go far enough. Certainly your interests and abilities are important, but using this information alone is limited. The limitation is caused by the fact that these aspects of our character change over time! So as we age and gain experience, it is natural to find new interests. As our abilities grow with time, we value these skills differently. This shift is a natural phenomenon of aging. Therefore, the logical solution is to find the attributes about ourselves that ***don't*** change over time.

Do What You Are Because It's Who You Are

Each of us is born with a distinct and unique personality type. Our personality type is formed very early in life and changes little as we age. So, the secret is to discover what truly makes you happy and understand "the real you." This makes career selection a more natural and comfortable feeling because you deeply understand what is most important to you. This method is effective because people don't change their basic personality traits. So, how do we find out who we are? We'll show you how to do this in step one of the Right Fit™ Program using personality type indicators.

Chapter Two:
"the solution"

The Right Fit™ Program

The Right Fit™ Program is an easy to follow seven-step program that will help your student attend the right college for them and spend less money doing it. We have done the heavy lifting for you and simplified the whole process into these straightforward steps.

1. Personality Typing
2. Career Assessments
3. Career Research & Job Shadowing
4. Major & Minor Identification
5. College Search
6. Visits, Refine College List
7. Apply, Accept and Matriculate

Far too often, college is presented as a complicated process, but it's really not if you know what is truly important. There are dozens of books written by former admissions officers telling you how to get into the college of your dreams. And guess what happens? Students do get in, but is it the right college at the best price? The statistics indicate that something is very, very wrong. According to the U.S. Department of Education, National Center for Education Statistics, May 2005, "The Road Less Traveled," over 60% of students do not graduate from the original college they chose and 63% of students at 4 year public universities and institutions have not graduated by the end of their 4th year. In fact, about 22% of students are taking more than 6 years to graduate! So, students really don't have a big problem getting in, but they do have a big problem getting into the *right* school and finishing on time. The Right Fit™ Program will illustrate what you need to correct this. It is critical that you follow each step in the exact order shown. Selecting a college can be fun; but to achieve the best result, you must follow these steps in the correct order because each step is dependent on the one that came before it.

Step One: Personality Typing

Personality testing is the most overlooked step in the process and most misunderstood, yet it is one of the most critical for the college process. First, understand that personality typing is not aptitude testing. It's not just about what a student may excel in, but rather, guiding a person to help them understand the unique and fundamental properties of who they are as a person. The great news is this process doesn't take a lot of time or money. In fact, if you are highly motivated to do this step on your own, you can start with the book " Do What You Are," by Paul D. Tieger and Barbara Barron-Tieger, Third Edition, Little, Brown and Company, 2001.

When we are younger, we tend to like what we are good at – it gives us a sense of accomplishment, however, it does not <u>always</u> lead to a successful career choice. The fact is our interests and skills change over time. However, our personality type – the way we view the world and make decisions, remains highly consistent throughout our lifetime. Your unique personality type is a reliable indicator of your preferences both now and in the future. Also, 60 years of research has shown that you can measure a person's type reliably and consistently over time. This makes personality typing a highly valuable tool that we can use to help guide our children.

I know a talented engineer who learned the hard way that talent and happiness are very different. During high school, this young man had an excellent math teacher that he admired and bonded with. In fact, the teacher had such confidence in the kid, that he was called upon daily to explain solutions and "teach" the class math lessons. Consequently, he loved math class and got great grades. Encouraged by his good grades, the young man met with his high school guidance counselor concerning college. The parents were not well off financially and there was no money for college so the guidance counselor recommended that the student speak with an Air Force recruiter who he knew was looking for students with strong math backgrounds. Well, the recruiter and the student met, and the recruiter had great news for the student. The Air Force would offer this bright kid a full ROTC scholarship to Penn State (lots of cute girls and a great football team!) if the student was interested in pursuing an Electrical Engineering degree. And to top it off, he may even get the chance to fly jets!

So, guess what this young man did? He graduated from Penn State, got his Master's degree in Electrical Engineering, and became an engineer. A decade later, he was absolutely miserable. That's right; he discovered that he hated being an engineer. The good news was his parents didn't have to pay for the education (the taxpayers footed the bill), but the bad news was that it cost him ten years of his life. I know this man, very well in fact, because the young man I'm writing about is me. Today, I'm a college counselor with a Master's degree in Electrical Engineering. Thirty years ago, if I had the benefit of personality typing, I would have learned that I am naturally suited for advising and educating people. The moral of the story is: do not over look personality testing. Typing will identify those careers that are good matches for your student. Remember, being good at math did not make me an engineer. Loving aviation did not make me a fighter pilot. I really am and always will be a teacher by personality – and finally today, I teach families about the college process. I learned it's not always about our talents, but rather who we are and how we want to spend each day. Now let's discuss the most widely recognized and utilized tool for personality typing, the MBTI®.

MBTI®

Discovering your personality type is both easy and fun. We believe that one of the best methods for doing so is the Myers Briggs Type Indicator (MBTI®). The MBTI® is a straight forward and simple method to help anyone get a clear understanding of what they prefer. This concept was first introduced in 1921 by Swiss psychologist Carl Jung and later refined by Katharine Briggs and her daughter, Isabel Briggs Myers. Today, this indicator has evolved from Jung's early work and has withstood many years of scrutiny. I know of no other technique that has been studied more than the MBTI®. Research has found this tool to be both reliable and valid when properly administered by a qualified counselor.

It is important to understand what the indicator is and what it is not. <u>It is not a way to pigeon-hole someone into a particular career.</u> The MBTI® does not determine intelligence or predict success. It does not make judgments about one person's preferences as compared to another. Rather it simply measures what your preferences are. In other words, it is completely non-judgmental. This is especially critical when using this indicator with the often hyper-sensitive state of your teenager. Different people of the same personality type can have different backgrounds, experiences, interests, and so on. In fact, this indicator has nothing to do with *directly* selecting a career at all. Rather, it helps a person to clearly understand those attributes that motivate and energize them. It helps people discover the critical aspects of their personalities that won't change over time, and in turn, gives them the power to seek out these elements in the work they choose. For those of you who have some experience with the MBTI®, we would like to caution you that we recommend a specific version of the MBTI® designed specifically for high school students. The indicator commonly administered to adults, typically in a work place environment, is not suitable for high school students.

The MBTI® saves the most in terms of money and time because the student gains a clear understanding of his or her innate personality traits. Knowing oneself is the key. Parents of my generation have a tendency to believe that everybody is destined to change careers several times. National statistics support this belief; however, it's also no surprise that these same people never went through professionally administered career planning or The Right Fit™ Program. I sometimes hear a parent say: "Teenagers are too young to know what they want." My response is, "That is exactly why this program is so powerful." After all, it's about doing better for our children and guiding them to the best possible outcome: a happy life.

Understanding Your Type Helps in College Too

I remember clearly my daughters' first day of school and watching them board that big yellow bus with great trepidation. The truth is I was more nervous than they were. That seems like such a long time ago and in a few months my wife and I will drop off our twins for their first day of college. College is a life-changing event for both parents and students. One of the very best gifts a student can receive is clear understanding of their personality type preferences. This will help them to not just survive in college but to thrive in college. This is true whether the student is going to attend a two-year college, a four-year college or a trade school. Knowing their preferences and MBTI® results will help them identify their own unique learning style, as well as how to better communicate with professors, roommates and friends.

Several colleges today require students take the MBTI® type indicator as part of orientation and use the results to match roommates. These colleges have had excellent results with fewer students requesting a change of roommate. "Introduction to Type in College" by John DiTiberio and Allen Hammer (pg 13) explored one such case. "At one college, a year after pairing students by similar type, researchers found that requests for roommate changes had fallen by 65%." DiTiberio and Allen also found that "students paired with similar types said they were more satisfied, while pairs of opposite types had lower overall GPAs." If you've ever had a bad roommate, you know how stressful it can be when you don't get along. A student's MBTI® results will also help them to understand their own unique learning styles. For example my daughters have absolutely no problem studying while listening to music or with background noise. Both my wife and I on the other hand need an absolutely quiet environment for us to be able to concentrate. Neither my wife nor I would make a good roommate for either one of our twin daughters. Another powerful use of MBTI® is helping your student understand the differences between their own learning styles and how college professors teach. Large-scale studies have been done that show the teaching styles of most college professors differ significantly from the learning styles of most college students. Understanding this ahead of time will help your student to better cope with the college learning environment.

Personality Type Resources

The best way to determine your personality type is to hire a certified professional trained to both administer the indicator and to assist with the verification of the results. However, if you would like to try it on your own, start with the following books:

1. "Do What You Are," Paul D. Tieger & Barbara Barron-Tieger, Little, Brown and Company, 2001.
2. "Career Coaching Your Kids," David H. Montross, Theresa E. Kane, Robert J. Ginn, Jr., Davie-Black Publishing, 2004.
3. "Introduction to Type in College," John K. Ditiberio, Alan L. Hammer, CPP, Inc., 1993.

Step Two: Career Assessments

As parents we tend to get that nice warm fuzzy feeling when our child passionately states they know exactly what they want to be for the rest of their lives. We naturally tend to avoid questioning the decision. Why rock the boat? Why kill the dream? When our child feels the passion, we think it's great because it means that they know exactly which career is right for them. We have all heard it: "Do what you love and you'll never work a day in your life." That's the mantra. But is it true? The answer is: maybe.

Recently, a very bright young man came in with both of his parents. He presented his 3.9 GPA and a long list of outside activities in various clubs with great pride. He was mildly concerned about finding the right college but seemed confident that he could do that himself the summer between his junior and senior years. I asked him if he knew what he wanted to study. His answer was clear and absolute – he wanted a career in politics and would study political science in college. He was absolutely convinced that this was the right path for him. The parents were beaming with pride at their 17 year old's confidence and certainty. So naturally, I asked this bright young person what made him so certain. He stumbled only slightly but quickly stated that he was fascinated with the political process and reading about the history of politics. He also enjoyed working with his fellow students during various club activities, in particular organizing and participating in group projects. Next came the moment of truth: I asked him what he thought it was about *his personality* that made politics such a good fit. He did not know except to restate that he really loved the subject.

So, what would you do as a parent? Would you go with the flow or ask your child to look a little deeper? This young man could be headed for a long, successful and rewarding career. He could be headed for a disaster. At the tender age of 17, how can anyone be so confident? Well, this student could be on the right track if he knew what it is about his personality that was driving him toward the choice. Additionally, it is always important to do as much career shadowing as possible to help verify a particular career choice, especially when there is no experience to base the decision on. This young man does have a picture in his head of what being a politician means and what he actually wants to pursue is *that* vision. But what happens if his vision doesn't match reality, and how long will it be before he actually realizes it? What can any 17 year old, no matter how bright, really know about a particular career unless they have looked deeper than a textbook or a high school club. Real career planning is a very practical and powerful scientific approach to help a student become clear about their motivations. If this young man is truly on the right path, then career counseling will help him verify his choice, it will become brighter and more defined for him. If he is less suited, then he gets to see this sooner rather than later.

The conundrum for parents is to avoid killing our children's dream once we have added in a heavy layer of practicality to their vision. The answer is you never, ever kill the dream. You let your student alter their dream (if needed) after consideration. If they make the decision, chances are they are more likely to follow through with it. Career counseling will clarify and enhance a person's vision and it makes their dream clearer because it adds sound reasons as to why it is the right path. Please give this careful thought as you guide your student.

Step Three: Career Research & Job Shadowing

During this step your student will begin searching for a career or several careers that make sense <u>based</u> on the personality typing results. The key is to look deeply into each career and cross-reference the personality preferences with career characteristics that meet as many of the preferences as possible. Assessments that include students' interests, abilities and values are also evaluated and will yield additional information to compare with the personality preferences. These are the most prevalent assessments used by your high school guidance counselors. Often called "aptitude" assessments, these tests seek to identify what your child has a current interest or ability in. Just remember abilities and interests change. It is important to use these in conjunction with personality profiles in order for the student to understand the pros and cons of each career possibility based on their personality (which won't change). Before narrowing the career choices, it is imperative that some research be done. It is important for a student to understand the details regarding each potential career such as: day-to-day tasks, education requirements, travel, salary, etc.

Most students come to us with very unrealistic ideas about the day-to-day life in a career. I'm sure that there are career counselors all over the country that hate the TV show "CSI." You may be laughing, and if you have teenagers you probably know where I am headed with this. It is truly frightening how many students cite TV shows when we ask them why they are interested in a particular career. For adults, we understand all too well that what happens on TV rarely mimics real life jobs, but for many students, TV is their only frame of reference. I have also had students come in and be convinced they are going to be a doctor. My first response is to talk about the requirements that must be fulfilled before they will be able to practice. Most are aware of medical school, and the severity of time and work they will have to put in for that. But a funny thing often happens when I start talking about internships and residencies. Most students have no idea that, on top of the six or seven years to get out of medical school, they will have to spend multiple years working long shifts before they can branch out into their field of choice.

Another common issue we face is a student's lack of knowledge when it comes to money. Most students don't have any idea how much their parents make or, more importantly, how much they have to spend to run their household. Have an open conversation with your child. I understand you may not want to tell them all your financial details, but please give them an idea of how much money it takes to maintain the lifestyle they are accustom to living. The point is, students need adults to give them information (whether they like it or not). You may be thinking, my child won't listen to me. This is an ideal opportunity to use a third party to bridge the communication gap. We often give students a piece of advice or an instruction that their parents have already given them. Yet what happens? They ignore their parents and listen to us. They are not trying to make you miserable. It is a natural stage of development. Teenagers must break from their parents in order to move into adulthood. This is why working with a professional comes in handy so often during this process.

Once the careers have been narrowed down, it's time go out into the world and spend some time on the job. Nothing gives a better perspective than spending a few hours with someone carrying out their daily activities. Job shadowing is a great way to eliminate big mistakes. A great example is my daughter, Vivian. Vivian is a straight A student with a strong background in biology and statistics. She also has demonstrated a strong personality type preference for helping and serving people. In short, she wants to use her strong science and math background to help others. So it seemed to make sense that her initial career choice was to pursue pharmacy. The next step was to send Vivian out into the real world and spend a few hours testing her hypothesis. Both my wife and I were very excited to learn that she was interested in pharmacy because pharmacists make well over $100,000 to start. To us, the cost of an undergraduate degree seemed to make a lot more sense with the prospect of our daughter making a starting salary in the neighborhood of six figures. Unfortunately for mom and dad, this simply was not to be. After Vivian spent a few hours with a real pharmacist, observing the day-to-day tasks, she decided that it definitely wasn't for her. Of course, we asked why. Our daughter explained to us that what she observed was a lot of administration: phone calls, counting out pills and making labels.

There is an important lesson here. A deeper look into what was motivating Vivian and her desire to help people revealed that what she was really looking for was a more personal relationship with those she helps. She learned that day she would not be happy counting pills and answering phones. She instead needs the more direct physical contact with those she serves. So it makes perfect sense that after her visit with the pharmacist, she has now decided to pursue a career in physical therapy. Think about all the time, heartache, and money that we saved by finding this out today and not 10 years from now. The reality is that when a young person says they're interested in a particular career, what they really mean is that they're interested in what they perceive to be true about that career. Ultimately, career satisfaction will be directly related to the accuracy of that perception. This is why career shadowing is a necessary step in the Right Fit™ Program.

If you miss this step, it usually hurts down the road, just ask my wife, Terri. Some 30 years ago, my wife was a teenager trying to decide what she should major in at Penn State. She has always been very close to her mother and greatly respects her mom's advice. Having known her mom for almost 30 years, I would have to agree that she does have excellent judgment. Terri sat down with her mom to discuss selecting a college major. Terri was unsure so she asked her mom what she thought would make a good career. Her mother explained that there were not a lot of women in the insurance industry and that she knew several people who did very well financially in insurance. The icing on the cake was that Penn State University had an insurance designation as part of the business school. So my future wife entered the business school and received her BS in business with a minor in insurance. Subsequently, she went on and received the professional designation of Chartered Property Casualty Underwriter (CPCU). Well, her mom was right. As it turned out they were not many women in the insurance business and even fewer had their CPCU Designation, so Terri did quite well and 10 years into her career, she was making over $100,000 per year.

Unfortunately for us both, Terri was miserable. Why? Because the day-to-day tasks as an insurance executive simply did not match the innate fundamentals of my wife's personality, such as helping others and developing a connection with the people around her. If you asked her today what she should have been, she'll tell you point blank that she should have been a grade school teacher. Just for fun, Terri has completed a personality typing profile. At the very top of the list of good matches is grade school teacher. I believe this story is poignant for parents. I know as the father of three daughters, I feel in many ways I know them better than they know themselves. Although this is probably true, the fact is what I know about them is completely irrelevant when it comes to planning their careers. **The only thing that matters is what your child knows about themselves.** That's what they will follow through with, and ultimately, that's what will make them happy. Even the most loving, well-intentioned parents may not be the best person to advise their own children when it comes to career planning. I will let you decide this for yourself. I think it's telling that in the medical profession, physicians consider it malpractice to operate on a loved one or a close friend. I believe career planning is just as important.

I recently had a very telling experience with a family who visited me in my office. The mother and father brought their eighth grader in to discuss the Right Fit™ Program. I asked the young man if he knew what he wanted to pursue as his career. He glanced briefly at his parents and then turned to me and said that he would like to be a doctor. I explained to this very bright and articulate eighth-grader that our program involves doing career counseling first and subsequently using that information to select majors and colleges. After I was done explaining our program, the young man became very excited. He exclaimed "so I could learn about my personality first and then if there was something that was a better fit for me than being a doctor, I can do that instead." It warmed my heart to realize that this eighth-grader understood our program perfectly. Unfortunately for him, his parents both looked like they were going to have a heart attack when they heard his statement. Seeing his parents' reaction, I asked them what they did for a living. By now you've probably guessed the answer. Dad is a cardiologist and mom is a homemaker.

Clearly these two parents are more concerned about <u>their</u> vision of what their son should be. Now please don't misunderstand me, I have no idea if this young person is well-suited to being a physician. But neither do his parents. As parents, sometimes we simply don't realize how much influence we have over our children. Even when we think our children are not listening to us, they actually are. It's very important that when a young person selects their major that they are truly the ones who are doing the choosing. When an impressionable teenager doesn't really know what they want to do, sometimes they will simply choose to please us. This is why personality typing and career planning are so very critical. They allow the student to do meaningful self exploration prior to major selection.

Step Four: Major & Minor Identification

Selecting the major will be a natural outcome of following Steps One, Two and Three. Sometimes the right major will be obvious and sometimes there may be a little research required. You may need to dig deep into various college course offerings to find the gem. In other words, check the course lists for programs you think you are interested in. See if the classes match the career you have in mind. Sometimes this digging will lead to something unexpected. An example is our daughter, Phebe. Phebe happens to be interested in Psychology as a field of study – with a focus on therapy/counseling and helping people in a one-on-one setting. She also happens to be an extremely talented artist. Our search found several top universities that have Master's Degree Programs in "Art Therapy." What an excellent way to combine Phebe's personality, interests, and skills into a single major.

In our experience, we have found that some students will need a little more time to get completely comfortable with their career choice and that's where Step Four can be very helpful. This step can provide your student with the opportunity to select a minor/major pair that will ease their mind. Let me explain with an example. We recently received a request for help from a distraught parent whose oldest son, now a junior in college, still didn't know what he wanted to do upon graduation. We agreed to meet with the young man and it became immediately apparent to me that this was a very intelligent and hard-working person. But you wouldn't know it by looking at his college transcript. Why? Because it showed he was behind in credit hours and was receiving mostly C's and to top it off, he didn't know why he was studying the particular courses he was taking! He was lost, behind in credit hours needed to graduate and on the verge of dropping out. In other words he didn't really know what his major should be because he didn't really know what he wanted to do with the rest of his life. The only reason he was still in college was because he felt a strong obligation to his parents – lucky for him, he has solid family support.

We recommended the student complete personality typing and career assessments. This young man was a very productive and active person, holding down several jobs as well as being very active athletically. In short, he was not a lazy person. So why was he doing so poorly and how had he lost his way? The reason is simple and it happens to many young people. This young man was a very hands-on person, very down-to-earth and practical. So for him, it was not easy to make the connection between the types of things you learn in a classroom and what really happens on the job. In a nutshell, this was his dilemma. As it turns out, his personality type was an excellent match for several career fields in which he was both interested in and suited for. He also had a particular personality type like many people, in which he simply preferred to keep his options open. And because he liked to keep his options open, making a final "life or death" decision on a career was stressful for this young man. So the solution was to develop a major/minor combination that would not force him to feel he was making a *final* decision. In other words, he got to keep his options open. He ultimately agreed to major in business management with a minor in finance. This was a great fit for him. The key to removing stress came from his understanding that he preferred to keep his options open, and that he didn't easily make the connection between theory in the classroom and practice on the job.

This made it easier for him to sit through those classes because he understood what the end goal was. He was then free to pursue his ultimate goal without feeling pigeonholed. This is an excellent example of how helping a young person to understand themselves better by recognizing their natural innate preferences can put them back on the right path. This young man's mother made it clear to us that if we had not intervened, he was on his way to dropping out of college completely.

One of the most common requests for help that we receive is from parents who are very concerned because their student doesn't know what they want to major in. Actually this can be a great place for a student to begin. Sometimes it's easier to know those things that you don't want to do when you're 17 years old. Either way, it's critical to complete personality typing at this point because it is a proven method to help the student get clear on which careers are going to be good fits. Sometimes it's much more troubling when a high school student tells us that they are absolutely certain on a particular career. This usually means the student has formed a very concrete vision of what they think they should be. In some instances this is based on a sound understanding of who they are, but in most cases, it's not.

A few years ago I had another very poignant "what major are you interested in?" discussion with a family. Both parents and the student were in my office when I turned to the student and asked him what he thought he would like to major in. With great confidence he turned to me and replied "computer animation and gaming design." This high school junior had clearly given his choice considerable thought. After a few more questions, the young man left the room and went across the hall to begin his personality assessment. That left mom, dad and me alone in my office. The minute the young man left my office, the parents broke out in shocked exclamation at what their son had just told me. Apparently, the father had left a well-paying job up north and moved the entire family to Florida expressly so that their son could pursue his dream: to be a marine biologist! In fact, the whole family earned their Master Scuba Diver certifications with many deep dives under their belt. Their son's interest in computers was a complete shock to them. Apparently their son was simply too embarrassed to tell his parents that he had experienced a change of heart. In the privacy of the next room, the young man confided in one of our career counselors that awhile back in one of his high school labs he was forced to dissect a frog. This experience made him realize that cutting open amphibians or for that matter fish was not something that he wanted to ever experience again. In short, he did not have the stomach to be a marine biologist. As it turned out, his personality assessment revealed that computer programming is an excellent career fit for this young person. It has been our experience that often times teenagers will reveal their deepest feelings and desires with our career counselors. This young man wasn't trying to deceive or hide anything from his parents, he just felt terrible that he had changed his mind.

Step Five: College Search

My wife's younger sister Debbie has always been a high-energy, outgoing people person. She is the classic definition of someone who shows a strong preference for extroversion. In other words, she draws her energy from being around other people. Debbie was quite popular in high school and a standout field hockey star, so it was natural for her to follow many of her friends and attend West Chester University located right in her hometown of West Chester,

Pennsylvania. It was during a weekend road trip to the main campus of Penn State to visit her sister Terri (my future wife), that Debbie decided it was time for her to move up to the big time. Subsequently she decided to transfer from West Chester University to Penn State. Basically she saw all the fun and good times her older sister was having and she decided that West Chester University was simply too small for her. Being an extrovert, her decision seemed logical and sound at first. She subsequently transferred to Penn State but she was surprised when she had difficulty with the transition. Why? Because she had become accustomed to the warm intimate environment of a much smaller campus and at Penn State's main campus (30,000 plus inhabitants) she initially felt somewhat overwhelmed and lonely. It wasn't until she joined a sorority that she really began to settle down and feel comfortable again. Fortunately for Debbie, she has the type of personality that is highly adaptable and very success orientated. In fact, she went on to become an extremely successful sales executive in the air freight business.

Unfortunately, many students would not be able to make this kind of transition successfully. Remember that 60% of students don't finish where they began. So how do most families actually pick colleges? Many students don't really conduct a true college search at all, instead they consider just those colleges that they've heard about (or their high school counselor tells them about). In fact, that is exactly what Debbie did when she initially selected West Chester University. Over 70% of students end up attending an in-state public university. This type of myopic approach results in a tremendous loss of time, energy and money. Exhibit 1 is from a class I teach on college and career planning, and when I show this to attendees it generally gets a big laugh. Unfortunately the reason it's funny is because it's also true. Although the teenage years naturally put a strain on the communication between parents and kids, college needs to be the exception. It's simply too big of a decision to be made by only one member of the family. Open and honest communication, however difficult, is the best way to pick the right universities to apply to. We have found the most successful parents were able to find a common ground with their kids – even if the final selection was not the student's or parents' first choice initially. Teenagers often make their initial selection based on less than rigorous criteria. For instance, it's the school where all my friends are going, it's my parents Alma Mata, it's a party school or it has a good football team (that one got me). All of these are lousy ways to pick something as important as college. The goal is to make the college selection decision a partnership between the parents and the student.

Exhibit 1

How students and parents pick

Students:	Parents:
■ Boyfriend	■ Money
■ Girlfriend	■ Money
■ ALL of my friends	■ Money
■ It's a party school, but don't tell my dad	■ Quality of Education
■ Good sports teams	■ I went there
	■ Any school within a two hour drive

Source: Kenneth Albert 2009 College Class

As an alternative to using the criteria above, Exhibit 2 shows a more scientific approach to building your list of college candidates.

Exhibit 2

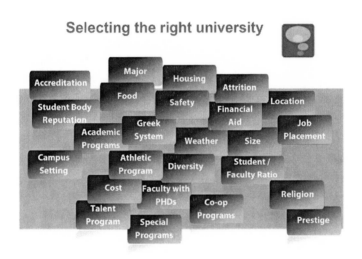

Source: Kenneth Albert 2009 College Class - *Note: You can view the entire presentation at www.KennethAlbert.com

There are a great number of free sites on the web that will allow you to input the variables that are important to you and create a list. When researching colleges, we have found a few books that give useful information. The *Student's Guide to Colleges: the Definitive Guide to America's Top 100 Schools* is written by students for students. The book gives an unbiased view of schools, where actual students give candid answers to questions like "What won't you see on a college tour?", "What will an admission's officer not tell a prospective student?" and "What is the education and social scene really like?" and more. *Colleges That Change Lives* by Loren Pope is a review of some of the most overlooked values in higher education. You should be warned that this book presents a scathing review of the Ivy League schools. Basically, Pope's position is that the Ivy League's are overrated, bloated institutions that represent a poor value in higher education. Pope also takes a dim view of overcrowded public universities as well. Of course, there is always the ever popular U.S. News & World Report listing of the best colleges. The problem with all of these sources is that they're really just big lists of data. Although the data serves a purpose and is useful to a certain extent, it is also misleading to say that one college is better than another.

Research clearly shows that different students can and do have a very different experience at the same institution. There is more variability within the learning experience at a particular institution than exists from institution to institution. Any attempt to quantify and rank one institution against another is a farce. For example, 25% of the U.S. News & World Report rankings depend upon a school's reputation as reported by surveys of college administrators. Further, the 2008 survey was only returned by 51% of administrators. How much does an administrator in the state of Florida really know about the quality of education at a university located in California or in Pennsylvania? Most of the people being surveyed have never even visited the campus they are ranking.

It's unfortunate that the popularity of these rankings is causing some institutions to play the game by actively seeking freshman characteristics that will move them up in the rankings. But think about this for a minute: if your student attends a university where the average incoming freshmen SAT scores are 50 points higher than the national average, what impact will this have on the quality of education that your child receives? The answer is none. The quality of the education that your child receives has very little to do with the type of information that you're going to find in this type of ranking. All of these sources fail to reveal the actual learning environment and the actual learning experience that your student will be exposed to. A better way to evaluate the quality of higher education is to focus on the quality of **teaching** and **learning** as opposed to "reputation," university resources, and the average SAT scores of incoming freshmen.

Often students and parents will ask me which universities are best in research. I usually respond with "Why do you ask?" The most common answer is because the student is interested in conducting research as an undergraduate. The harsh reality is that faculty members at research universities are there to do research not teach. But your child is going there to be taught. Do you see where this is going? Often times, these faculty have been recruited to the institution with the promise of not being burdened with teaching! It is common for certain faculty to have been promised, for example, that they will only teach one or two classes with most of the student contact being handled by adjuncts or teaching assistants. This is a good deal for the professor because they can stay focused on the research, but it's clearly a bad deal for your child.

Ironically, many of the so-called top ranked schools suffer from this affliction. A fascinating article appeared in The Chronicle of Higher Education, "On the Bottom Line, Good Teaching Tops Good Research," by Frank Heppner, an honors professor at the University of Rhode Island. The article is based on his observations over 40 years. He laments that too much emphasis is placed on the pursuit of research grants as compared to the teaching of undergraduates, "a glance through our campus phone book reveals 38 names associated one way or another with grant acquisition or processing (compared with two names associated with the improvement of teaching)." This man teaches honors classes, so he understands students who care about how they are taught and what they learn.

When describing instructional-development programs designed to improve teaching, he states, "These offices are typically marginalized and token at research universities, without appropriate money, prestige or appreciation. Faculty members typically have no official incentive to seek advanced training in teaching; in fact, they are often discouraged because of the disproportionate emphasis placed on research productivity." He makes a compelling argument that colleges could actually increase their net revenues by focusing on student learning and less on grant acquisition. I agree. Students respond differently and produce wonderful outcomes when they feel their professors actually care about *them*. As parents, we need to know how a university is approaching this issue. The good news is, some colleges are truly student-focused and I will show you how to find them.

What sort of information can you trust about the quality of **teaching** and **learning** actually going on in college? If you ask students who they trust the most for information about a particular institution they will answer: students at those institutions. I agree. One of the best sources of information about a college is found by asking those who have experienced it firsthand. However, in the past this type of information was impossible to find. This is changing.

In 1999, a small group of researchers conducted a pilot study of 13 colleges with the goal of assessing and improving the quality of undergraduate education. They have done this through a series of professionally crafted surveys known today as the National Survey of Student Engagement (NSSE). The surveys ask both freshmen and seniors a series of questions designed to provide the institution with data they can use to improve all students' experience at the college. The primary focus is on the quality of teaching and student outcomes. Examples of quality teaching and student outcomes include graduating within four years, doing undergraduate research, timely feedback from professors and preparation for graduate level work. As of 2008, more than 1300 colleges and universities have participated and the latest report is available on their website (www.nsse.iub.edu). The website is a treasure trove of information and I highly encourage you to visit it. The goal of the research is to produce meaningful and measurable improvements in the quality of post secondary education by measuring student engagement and subsequently providing feedback to participating institutions. The series of surveys are very detailed, as well as professionally developed and administered with the ultimate goal of that information being used by the colleges themselves as a method to improve their students' experience.

The "experience" includes measuring student outcomes like the quality of instruction received, which has a direct bearing on metrics like graduating on time. NSSE makes it very easy for colleges to participate in the surveys because they do all the work including providing a series of reports back to each college at a low cost. The college is free to use the feedback as they see fit. Some institutions have definitely embraced the intent and spirit of this work and are using it to improve the student learning experience. The bad news is that it took until the year 2000 for colleges to finally come around and measure those things that actually matter, but the good news is they are finally doing it. It appears now that the National Survey of Student Engagement has got legs and I believe that in the future it may become a standard measure of quality.

It is important to note that the NSSE is adamantly opposed to using this information as a means to <u>rank</u> one college against the other. They do not want this to turn into another "arms race" for rankings the way US News and World Report has become. The goal is to obtain, analyze and disseminate accurate data to improve higher education, not to pit one institution against another. Supporting this view, their research shows that student experiences and outcomes vary more from student to student than they do from college to college. For example, Student A can have an excellent experience at College A while at the same time Student B can have a poor experience at College A. Furthermore, The National Survey of Student Engagement has agreed that it will keep the results of the surveys confidential and it is up to each institution to decide how and when and if at all, they make their particular results public. As a consumer of higher education this doesn't make me happy, but I understand why NSSE feels they have to do this. Again their goal is to help colleges improve student experiences and outcomes, and obviously certain institutions would be reluctant to participate if they knew that their dirty laundry was going to be aired publicly.

The good news for parents and students is that some colleges are very happy to share the results with you. For instance, check out Elon University's website at www.elon.edu for an excellent presentation of their performance results compared to the NSSE benchmarks. I see a day in the not too distant future when college websites look like Elon's and the NSSE criteria become the standard that colleges use to report the quality of learning experienced on their campus. The key to understanding this research can be best understood by examining the benchmarks themselves. According to the NSSE, "The benchmarks are based on 42 key questions from the NSSE survey that capture many vital aspects of the student experience. The student behaviors and institutional features are some of the more powerful contributors to learning and personal development." I have included these five critical benchmarks in the appendix, however, I would encourage you to download "Promoting Engagement for All Students: The Imperative to Look Within, 2008 Results" and read the actual survey questions for a better understanding of the results.

What makes these benchmarks so powerful is the focus on the quality of teaching and the outcome of learning. In doing so, they move the discussion away from the flawed quality indicators like reputation, SAT scores or the football team. In the past, we have tended to think of educational quality as something attributed directly to an institution and that one college can be better than another. In fact, this is a false perception. The National Survey of Student Engagement is finally shining a light on this issue and has begun the march away from national rankings of "best colleges." Think about it. If you're a student trying to select a college, which information would ultimately have the most impact, the average SAT scores of classmates or what 380,000 randomly sampled students have to say about their <u>learning</u> experiences?

Step Six: Visits, Refine College List

Before you spend any time or hard earned money to visit a college, determine if they participate in the NSSE study. If they do not, you should ask why. The answer cannot be because it is expensive or because it is difficult to administer. The cost is only a few thousand dollars and NSSE does all the work. If they do participate in the NSSE surveys, then request the results. If the college refuses to share the results, why visit at all? If they do provide the results, you can review them and use this information as an additional tool when deciding which institutions warrant a visit. During the visit you should ask questions related to your students' field of study and ultimate goal (i.e. graduating on time, going on to graduate school, etc.). You should also ask questions related to strengths and weaknesses as seen in the NSSE results: "How is the college addressing the results of the NSSE survey response?" etc. If that isn't enough, here are some additional tips:

1. Sit in on a class or two (one freshman class and one in your major)
2. Talk to students (not just the one giving the tour)
3. Make appointments with an admission's officer, financial

aid officer and a professor from the program you are interested in

4. Visit the freshman dorms (don't assume the dorms they show you will be the ones you live in)

5. Eat in the cafeteria (parent weekends don't count – the food is always better during these times)

6. Check out the library. Is there anyone there? How up-to-date are the facilities?

Ask these questions:

1. What percentage of students in my major graduate in four years?

2. Will all my teachers be full professors with Ph.D.'s or terminal degrees?

3. What is the average class size for general education (required) classes? Major specific classes?

4. How often are students delayed from getting required classes?

5. What is your enrollment yield? (Number of students that matriculate divided by the number of admitted students.)

6. What are the campus safety procedures?

7. What are the admissions criteria and which are the most important?

8. What expenses do they include in the total cost of attendance? What expenses are not included?

9. What merit scholarships are available, and how do I apply for these? If there are additional forms to complete, when are the deadlines?

10. What is the average percentage of financial need met with scholarships/grants (free money)?

11. What is the average debt incurred by the time students graduate?

Most of the scheduled tours that colleges conduct are marketing pitches with information that you can generally find by searching their websites. However, you can get a general feel for the campus environment and local community. By combining the NSSE results and campus visits as I have outlined, you will yield the best results.

Step Seven: Apply, Accept, and Matriculate

The application is the main vehicle that colleges will use to ultimately decide whether or not your student will be admitted. Getting this step correct cannot be over emphasized. Keep in mind that a college admissions officer will spend maybe 15 to 20 minutes reading an application and any supporting documents. The decision will be made in those 15 to 20 minutes. It is critical that the application be well-organized, complete and accurate. Each college will have different requirements of the application, so the best way to approach this is to have all the information organized and at your fingertips as you work through each application. Initially you need to check and see if there are any colleges on your list that accept the Common Application. The Common Application is a standardized form used by many colleges. This will save time because you only have to fill out this application once. You can obtain a copy of the Common Application from your guidance counselor or online (www.commonapp.org). Here's a list of items you will need *before* you begin the application process:

- Unofficial high school transcript
- SAT and/or ACT scores
- A list of work experiences
- Your essay
- Letters of recommendations
- List of volunteer community service hours

- A list of leadership positions
- A list of honors and awards

Letters of recommendation are an extremely important part of the application and will generally have a strong influence on the admissions officer's decision. Typically a letter of recommendation should be written by a teacher, a high school guidance counselor, a member of the clergy, a professional or business person or a community leader. It's important to carefully consider who will write the letter of recommendation. Select someone who knows the student well. It's also important that the letter of recommendation not simply restate accomplishments that can be found in other areas of the application. The goal is to reveal who you are as a person and to shed light on the student's personality with information that cannot otherwise be found in the application data. It's perfectly acceptable to supply the writer with material beforehand and discuss what might be in the letter of recommendation. Some teenagers are reluctant to do this, but a little coaching here goes a long way to ultimately make this process a lot of fun for all involved. It's important to remind your teenager that most people are flattered when requested to write a letter of recommendation and it's incumbent upon the student to help the writer as much as possible.

It's important to stay organized and create a calendar of deadlines. Most college admission application deadlines will be in January or February of student's senior year however some are as early as October. We have seen schools start to accept applications in July before the student's senior year! Students who apply early have the advantage while those who wait until the last minute will not garner any favors from admissions personnel.

Application Timeline

End of Junior Year:

- Continue to prepare for and take standardized tests (SAT, SAT II, ACT, AP exams, etc.).
- Determine which 6-10 schools the student will apply to. Be sure to review the statistics of the common applicant pool (GPA, standardized tests, rank, etc.) and compare these with the student's own statistics.
- Complete a resume. This will require the student to collect and summarize all important information.
- Set up college visits. Try to meet with professors, admissions directors, financial aid counselors, students and academic advisors. Some colleges will allow students to spend a night in one of the dorm rooms to get a feel for the flavor of the campus. It is important to maintain contact with each school before and after the visits through phone calls and emails. Don't ask questions that can easily be found on the school's website.
- Request reference letters.
- Begin college application essays. In order to determine what the essay topics are, (and later fill out applications online); the student needs to visit each college's website and create an account. Normally this is as easy as starting a new application for admission. Remember, it is better to start online applications now. The student can always save the information and return later to complete it.
- Have at least two people review the rough draft essays.

Beginning of Senior Year:

- Complete online applications.
- Request your transcripts and collect any additional material needed for the applications (reference letters, counselor forms, resumes, etc.). Each school will have different requirements for the delivery of this information. Make sure to find out before you send things off. For example, some schools may only accept transcripts directly from the school. In this case, you should provide your school with stamped, addressed envelopes for each school. Similarly, some schools will only accept reference letters in a sealed (and sometimes signed) envelope.
- Continue contact with the admissions office to make sure they receive all the necessary paperwork and that no deadlines are being missed. Make sure to ask about housing and financial aid/scholarship forms and deadlines.
- Parents and students must work together to fill out all financial aid paperwork. FAFSA should be completed as soon after January 1st (during the senior year) as possible. CSS Profile forms have varying deadlines for each school.
- Continue to maintain (or better yet, exceed) grade trends. Colleges can revoke admission if grades drop.

When the admissions application is received by the college it will begin a process that is best described as secretive. Each college will score the application against a matrix of parameters that only that particular college is privy to. Unfortunately, knowing exactly how a particular college will weigh each of these parameters is not possible and can change from year to year. The best that you can do is to make sure that you are meticulous in following the college's instructions. Double check and have everything proofread by a second person. Understand how you are applying to each college, early action, early decision, or regular. Early *action* is non-binding. Early *decision* is a binding agreement. You may only select one college to apply as early decision and if that college admits you, you must attend. Think carefully about applying early decision. If you are required to attend, you forfeit your right to compare financial aid awards from other colleges. These definitions will help you through the process:

- **Regular admissions:** you apply for admissions under normal deadlines.
- **Rolling admissions:** you can apply for admissions at anytime during the year (up until classes start), and admission decisions are given out periodically during this period (rather than all at once).
- **Deferred admissions**: you can defer or postpone enrollment for up to one year generally for financial, personal or work-related concerns.
- **Early entrance**: you can be accepted and enrolled prior to high school graduation. A few colleges use this to attract better students.
- **Early decision**: you apply by an early deadline in order to enhance your chance of admission, but you are obligated to attend if admitted.
- **Early action**: you apply by an early deadline to enhance admission and you are *not* obligated to attend if admitted.

Apply to 6-10 colleges and let each college know where else you have applied. Put competition on your side. This must be an intelligently selected 6-10. Don't choose the large public college closest to you, a few more within a couple hours drive, and then throw in Harvard for kicks. You must follow the program, identify a career and major that fits you, then select colleges that offer that major and <u>compete</u> with each other. Your goal is to apply to as many colleges as practical where you are in the top 25% of incoming freshman. TIP: Colleges will require a tuition deposit no later than May 1 of your senior year and you can only send in one check. If you send in more than one, you run the risk of being rejected from them all.

Chapter Three:
"working within the system"

Who Decides?

Is it your intention to hand your teenager a $100,000 blank-check and have them fill in the name of the college? Think very carefully about the question, it's not as outrageous as it may first appear. I consistently read college articles that encourage you to "let the student decide," "your child must be the one to pick the college they will attend," blah, blah, blah. Do you know anybody of sound mind who would hand over $100,000 (or worse a loan obligation) to a teenager? I realize that every family dynamic is different and each parent makes their own decision as to how the college is ultimately selected. It is not my intention to dictate to any family how they approach this issue. It is your money and your child, and I know firsthand how emotional this issue is for both parents and students.

The most successful families start very early and clearly communicate to their child that mom and dad have an equal vote – everybody must compromise to select the final college to attend. The truth is, college selection is almost always a compromise, so start recognizing it early (9th grade) and communicate this to your child.

If you fail to do this, bad things can happen. For example, your child might visit a particular campus, fall in love with everything about it and ultimately get accepted only to find out that the financial award letter leaves a big hole. What will you do when this happens? Are you going to shatter your kids' dreams and explain the college they love isn't affordable? You are now in the exact position colleges hope you will be in. They know that most parents will do anything to make it work, which usually means raiding the retirement funds, taking high interest loans or stripping equity from the family home. Colleges spend most of their time and money marketing to *students*. The only solution to this issue is to be well prepared ahead of time. You need to be very clear with your child that some schools will not be financial fits unless a certain amount of merit or financial aid is received, no matter how much they like the school. Every student deserves to know that they can both succeed and be happy at a variety of institutions. There is no one perfect college for them.

What Do Colleges Really Want?

The most important factors colleges consider are your high school grade point average and class ranking. Highly selective universities may weigh the SAT/ACT very high, especially if they are looking to move up in the US News and World Report standings. Below is a comprehensive listing of what most colleges are looking for:

- High School Grades and GPA (with emphasis on curriculum)
- Class Rank
- SAT/ACT Scores
- Extra-Curricular Activities / Volunteer Work
- Special Skills and Abilities
- Letters of Recommendation

- Residency
- Diversity
- Interview Performance
- Student Interest in Their College

It's important to know that most colleges will calculate a unique GPA based on the rigor of your curriculum. For example, if you take honors classes or advanced placement classes, the college will recalculate your GPA and produce a new weighted GPA based on the difficulty of the courses you have taken. Generally speaking, it is more advantageous for students to receive a B in an honors class than to receive an A in a regular class. Also important to understand is why student interest matters to colleges. Colleges associate student interest with the student's excitement to attend that school. Most administrators equate a student's excitement about their school with the ability to succeed once a student is in attendance. So do your homework. Make calls, write emails and most importantly, visit each school you hope to receive merit aid from.

Advanced Placement Exams

By taking a standardized Advanced Placement course and exam, a student can assess their ability to handle first year college-level work. The college receives the same feedback when they review your scores. AP exams are graded on a scale of 1 to 5. A score of 3 is considered passing. Some kids hit 4's and even 5's and are obviously positioned to excel in college. But even a 1 or 2 score is still encouraging because it shows two things: first that the student is willing to challenge themselves by taking the course and second that they took the additional step of sitting for the exam. Most colleges rank advanced placement courses and exams very high on the list of qualifications. Students should review their academic strengths with their guidance counselor during 9th grade to determine which AP courses will benefit them. We also recommend that students consider additional AP courses based on their anticipated college major/minor. It is a potent admissions advantage when the AP courses are in harmony with the students' collegiate field of study.

Should You Take the SAT or ACT?

Each college will have their own specific requirements for these tests, so you must know early which colleges you will be applying to. Some will require either the SAT or ACT, and some may also require the SAT II subjects exams, which can also be specific to a major or program. The SAT has a verbal, math, and writing section, and penalizes students for wrong answers. The ACT adds in a science section and does not have a guessing penalty. Make sure to prepare in advance for the SAT, ACT and the PSAT/NMSQT. The PSAT is commonly thought of as the practice SAT. This is a mistake! The PSAT is the qualifier for National Merit Scholarships and often determines the level of college interest in your student early on in the process. We always recommend taking the SAT <u>and</u> ACT at least once. Once you take each test, you can decide which test you feel more comfortable with and can focus your efforts on that test alone, with prep courses and additional testing. If you do not score well on these types of tests, then you may consider some of the 800 colleges where the SAT/ACT is optional. Until colleges eliminate the SAT's, we still must play their game.

How Standardized Tests Affect Your Choice of Schools

All standardized testing is not created equal and some critics (such as Fair Test) of the SAT claim that the SAT is not predictive of college success beyond what can be ascertained from high school GPA and class rank. They have solid data to back it up. This is an epic battle between The College Board (they sell the SAT, SATII) and its supporters on one side and Fair Test (www.fairtest.org) and its supporters on the other. Both have arguments and data to support them. But for us mortals who are on the outside looking in at this debate, we need to keep our eye on the prize. As parents, our biggest concern is selecting the right college while also receiving sufficient scholarships and financial aid to make it affordable. This means your student must prepare and prepare diligently for these exams. There are excellent test preparation companies available to help. It has become quite popular lately for some (usually uninformed media types and high school guidance counselors) to recommend that students use free sources to prepare for the SAT/ ACT. For that rare student who is super self-motivated, this can work well; however, for most kids, this cheap way out will bear risk. We recommend that the students learning style be established as part of the personality typing and then match the student with the type of preparation service that best suits the student's learning style preferences. Your student must prepare for these exams because the competition is fierce. Let me explain.

My oldest two daughters are identical twins. They have resumes that are *almost* identical. They have the exact same number of community service hours doing the exact same service, they were on the exact same high school track team (and hold two school records), and they have the exact same GPA and are side-by-side in class rank. Yet despite this, when these two identical people were both accepted at The University of Miami, one received an *additional $32,000 in scholarship money*! I'm not kidding, $32,000 more for one "identical" kid compared to the other. We called the university in order to ascertain the reason for the difference, but they refused to give us any details. After some hounding on our part, we finally spoke to the Dean of Undergraduate Admissions. He pointed out that the one daughter's SAT scores were 20 points higher (out of a possible 1,600 points!). So, in this case *20 points is worth an additional $32,000*. And that made all the difference in affordability.

This brings up another important point. By the time we knew what the school was offering us, it was April. May 1st is the deadline for the decision. I asked the Dean to reconsider this decision and treat both daughters as equals. His answer was a definite "no." You will hear people say that you should negotiate with colleges to receive better awards. My position is that by the time you receive the award it may be too late. I want everyone to "pre-negotiate." You should select colleges that will want your student. Forget about "reach" schools. Everywhere I turn, I see advice telling students to choose two reach schools, two or three mid-range, and a couple safety schools. This will set your family up for disappointment and frustration! This advice comes from people who are entrenched in the current way of doing things. Obviously from the data I have shown, the current way does not work well for families and it only benefits the colleges.

It is important to explain a few definitions here. There are two types of reach schools. There are financial reach schools that the family cannot afford without merit aid from that school. This is a tricky area and I always recommend you speak to a professional to determine where your family really is as far as financial *need*. See the financial aid section of this book for more information. Your student's academics will determine whether they qualify for merit aid. You should have an up-front conversation with your student about these schools. They need to understand that unless the school gives your family the merit money needed, they cannot attend this school. Don't let your student fall in love with one school. Talking about this ahead of time helps manage expectations and can prevent heartache.

The second type of reach school is an academic reach. In other words, your student will be lucky if they are admitted. *Take these schools out of your list completely,* unless you have plenty of money to pay the entire cost of college flat-out (and are willing to do so). As previously expressed, there are multiple schools that will be the right fit for your student. Don't get caught up in the "brand name" hype surrounding some colleges.

It is important to know ahead of time where your student falls in each school's applicant pool. Try to be in the top 25% in regards to GPA, standardized tests, class rank, etc. Lucky for me, my kids followed The Right Fit™ Program and applied to 10 intelligently selected colleges. We have several other great choices that, by the way, offered my daughters exactly the same in scholarships and financial aid. Remember, some colleges are looking to move up in the US News and World Report standings and may deny your child's acceptance if their SAT score is just a few points below their cut-off for that year. Although it's not constructive to get mad, I would make your child understand this. The moral of the story is: prepare for the standardized tests and know where you stand.

As parents we need to keep things in perspective and help our kids understand that ultimately, their success and happiness in life will not be proportional to their SAT scores. It is also true for certain students these tests may be unfair. Why? Because these tests exclude some students from admission to certain institutions that are being manipulated by national rankings publications. In other words, if the average SAT scores for the incoming freshman class are higher at College A as compared to College B, then College A is ranked higher and receives a huge benefit. The fact is that a person's ability to excel in life cannot be measured by the type of tests that are being used today. Why do I believe this? First, I personally did not score high on the SAT's, yet I went on to earn my Master's degree in Electrical Engineering. Second, because colleges that have made the SAT optional, have <u>not</u> seen negative effects on student outcomes. And that is heart of the matter. Most of these tests only provide a snap-shot of what kids look like coming ***into*** college. And what we really care about is what kids look like coming ***out*** of college. The key is not to reject kids who may have the drive and character to succeed simply because they had a bad day one Saturday. So, if despite their best efforts, your child doesn't do as well as hoped on the SAT, please don't stress about it. The fact remains, there are many colleges that will both accept your child and be a good experience.

What's Wrong With the SAT?

According to College Board, (they produce the test) the SAT is supposed to be a good predictor of first year grades in college. However, the evidence to date shows that the SAT is lacking in its ability to provide any significant predictive powers above knowing a student's GPA and class rank. The SAT is only marginally helpful at predicting first year grades in college. Simply knowing high school grade point average and class rank is sufficient and very little is added by the SAT scores. The issue is: why are we continuing to put so much emphasis on a single exam, not to mention all the time, money and emotional energy that go into these exams, when the data clearly shows that the SAT adds little value to the process? Many good colleges have finally come around and no longer require these aptitude tests for admission.

Current research consistently shows that a student's first year *college* GPA is not significantly affected by their SAT scores. Consider that one of the nation's premier institutions, Wake Forest University, number 28 on the U.S. News and World Report list of top national universities, has recently announced that it will no longer require applicants to submit SAT or ACT scores. The University is joining a growing number of selective colleges in effectively throwing the SAT out the window. The president of Wake Forest, Nathan O. Hatch, said that an analysis of 2007 data "showed that colleges can attain both academic excellence and social diversity if they base admissions on high school grade-point average but not if they depend on SAT scores." This isn't news to Bates College, a top institution who has been SAT optional for 20 years. Bates policy shows statistically little difference in academic performance or graduation rates among students who choose not to submit SAT scores compared with students that did. Mount Holyoke College dropped the SAT requirement in 2001 and according to vice president for enrollment and college relations, Jane B. Brown, "The SAT does not add enough value for us to require students and their families to make such a large investment of time, energy, money in this single, high-stakes test." Mount Holyoke has conducted one of the most extensive research studies to date made possible by a $290,000 grant from the Mellon Foundation. The research found that the first year GPA of students who choose not to submit SAT scores was 3.24 while those who did submit were 3.35. Another landmark study, this one conducted by The University of California, Berkley and published in July, 2008, comes to the same conclusion. UC studied 125,000 students in the UC system between 1996 and 2001 and found that "the strongest predictor of college success was high-school grades in college preparatory courses." Further, they state "Irrespective of the quality or type of school attended, high-school GPA proved the best predictor not only of freshman grades in college, as many studies have shown, but also of long-term outcomes such as cumulative grade-point average and four-year graduation."

Most selective colleges as well as public universities show no signs of eliminating the requirement to submit SAT/ACT scores, so for now, the best advice is to be prepared for these exams. The exams are entrenched in part because they provide admissions personnel (who are awash in applications) with an easy, fast method to filter applicants. So if your scores are not what you think they should be, know that the scores have little bearing on long-term success. Remember, it is not possible for a single test to measure a person's desire, study habits or mental toughness to succeed and ultimately, those are the qualities that are most valued.

If you want to include colleges that don't require the SAT as part of your search, we have provided a sampling of several colleges that are SAT-optional in the appendix, along with a cross reference with U.S. News and World Report's 2009 college rankings. You can find a more extensive list at www.fairtest.org – a non-profit group that advocates an end to the SAT as a criterion for college admission.

Chapter Four:
"the money"

Financial Aid Nuts and Bolts

You will pay for college using one or a combination of the following:

A. **The federal government's money.** This can be free money such as grants and work study, or borrowed money in the form of government–backed loans. These funds are distributed through the institutions and it is each institution's responsibility to distribute these government funds.

B. **The institution's money**. Colleges use their endowment funds to attract the students they most want to enroll. Endowment funds may be in the form of tuition discounts, scholarships, or grants and are a reduction of the institution's cost of attendance.

C. **Private-sector money**. This is free money that will not have to be paid back and generally comes in the form of scholarships from clubs, organizations, and foundations. Private sector funding amounts to only about 3% of the total financial aid awarded annually.

D. <u>Private Loans</u>. This is currently the fastest growing segment of financial aid.

E. <u>Your cash flow and savings</u>. This will impact your future retirement.

As a general rule of thumb every family should apply for financial aid, regardless of income. Lower income families will generally receive grants and need-based scholarships from federal, state and college sources. Middle income families can generally expect to receive grants, scholarships, and federal loans if the student attends a private college. Upper income families will generally be offered federal student loans. Most students who attend college are eligible to receive some form of financial assistance. Money and scholarships are available to families of all income levels, but generally are offered by private universities. In most cases, very little merit money is offered by public institutions.

Cost of Attendance (COA)

Financial aid comes in two basic flavors: merit aid and need-based aid. Your real cost of attendance is used to calculate your financial need. COA includes:

- Tuition and fees
- Room and board
- Books and supplies
- Transportation
- Personal expenses

Merit-based financial aid is based on student attributes, in particular high school grade point average, ACT and SAT test scores and special talents, skills and extracurricular activities. The big money for merit-based financial aid is sitting in college endowment funds. Need-based financial aid comes in the form of federal grants, scholarships, loans and work study, and is based on what the government determines you should pay out of pocket for college. This is the formula for identifying if you qualify for financial aid:

Your Need = COA-EFC.

Will you qualify for financial aid? Here is a simplified formula:

Step 1. Determine the total cost of attendance by adding up all these costs:

- Tuition
- Dormitory
- Board
- Building fee
- Capital Improvement fee
- Student activity fee
- Health fee
- Parking fee
- Student service fee
- Technology fee
- Books
- Athletic fee

Step 2. Factor additional time to graduate based on 4, 5, and 6 year graduation rates.
Step 3. Your cost = step 1 amount + step 2 amount.
Step 4. Write the checks.

No, this is not meant to be funny. The reality is that 75% of families send their kids to public universities and unless your kid is a blue chip athlete playing on a revenue generating sport (football or basketball), you will receive little or no free money at a public university. You will, however, be offered loans and possibly work study because colleges consider both of these to be financial aid. For example, it is common for the average middle-class family to be offered either the Stafford (student loan), PLUS loans (a parent loan), or both. At rates of 6.8% and 8.5% respectively, these are great ways to significantly increase the cost of college. Most of the confusion comes from the fact that colleges think that by offering you loans, which somebody gets to pay back with interest, they have provided you with financial aid. Technically, they have. However, when parents ask me if they will get financial aid, they are thinking about money that they will not have to pay back. If you make a decent living, and your student attends a public university, the only thing you will be offered is loans. Many parents have heard about this and that is why I often hear the statement "I make too much money to get financial aid."

What's Your Expected Family Contribution (EFC)?

I mentioned before that your need equals the cost of attendance minus your EFC. Your EFC is what the government expects you to pay each year for the cost of college. It is computed using the parents' and the students' income and assets. It also takes into account the number of family members in the household and the number of your children who will be attending college in any particular year. The more students in college during the same year the less you are expected to pay. Unfortunately, parents are not included in this calculation so there is no benefit to having mom or dad take night courses in the attempt to lower their expected family contribution. Your expected family contribution will remain constant regardless of the cost of attendance. However, the government will lower your expected family contribution based on various living allowances, the amount of taxes paid by the family and the nature of certain assets.

The mathematical formulae which dictate how federal financial aid is delivered to the public are cumbersome and based on household finances of the 1950's era. The government has been posturing changes that would simplify this archaic system, however presently, the calculation is primarily driven by your income. For example, if a couple files a joint return with an adjusted gross income of approximately $95,000 per year, their expected family contribution would be approximately $18,000 per year. If your student was to attend the average public college or university that costs $18,000 per year, you will not qualify for any federal financial aid other than an unsubsidized Stafford loan. An unsubsidized Stafford loan is in the student's name and currently carries a 6.8% interest rate with payments to begin six months after the student graduates. However, the interest begins accruing immediately. Federal financial aid is not going to be of any help for most of us, unless you consider loans helpful. If by chance your EFC calculation is actually less than the cost of college per year, then you will have a demonstrated need. The problem is that some colleges will only meet a percentage of that need with free money, in other words grants, scholarships or tuition discounts. For example, if your EFC equals $10,000 per year and the cost of college equals $18,000 per year, then your need equals $8,000 per year. The college can choose to give you $8,000 in the form of a scholarship, $8,000 in loans, a combination of the two or nothing at all.

In many cases the financial aid officer will meet student needs with loans first and fill any remaining need with work study, grants and scholarships. The financial aid officer also has the option and many times will leave the family short. In other words, just because you qualify for financial aid doesn't mean that the college will meet 100% of your need. You can get an estimate of your EFC by accessing any number of free calculators on the web. These free calculators will not however, help you to lower your EFC and thus increase your need. Reducing your EFC is a complicated area that requires a complete analysis of your financial status. Additionally reducing your EFC may or may not benefit you and I have seen some cases where it can actually harm you.

Let me share an example with you. I was referred to a couple that had received the following advice from a so-called college advisor who was really just a salesman in disguise. The parents made about $100,000 per year, and had saved $36,000 in a custodial account (held in mutual funds) for their son to be used for college. The student had a 3.3 GPA and 1180 SAT score. This young man was happily on his way to the state public university at an annual cost of about $18,000 per year. The parents had two other kids to worry about and did not want to take debt for child number one, so they were concerned about how to finance college. Mom and Dad attended a college seminar from a local college "planner" and subsequently went to a free meeting in the advisor's office. The "planner" recommended that the parents sell the custodial account assets and transfer them into an annuity. The idea was to reduce their family EFC because, under the federal EFC formula, annuities are not counted. Custodial accounts in the child's name are counted at the rate of 20%. So, the idea was to reduce the EFC by .2 X $36,000 = $ 7,200. The idea is to hide the assets from the financial aid officer.

Well, the parents filed their FAFSA form on-line and got back their EFC immediately. They were shocked to see their EFC was equal to $18,657! This means that the move did absolutely nothing for them in terms of qualifying for Federal financial aid. They are expected to pay $18,657 and the college that their student will actually attend is only $18,000, no need here. They did however have to pay capital gains tax on the sale of the investments (all in the first year) and they also paid an 8% penalty to withdraw the funds from the annuity because they needed the money to pay for college. The only person who made any money on this deal was the insurance agent ("college advisor") who sold them the annuity. Be careful out there.

It is also true that in some rare cases, moving assets may provide financial aid benefits, but only if it will result in an EFC that is _below_ the cost of attendance. Even then, no benefits may accrue if the college decides to simply "gap" your kid and not make up the difference with financial aid. Remember, just having a need doesn't guarantee you will receive additional aid. It is my position that any financial transaction should be suitable based on its own merits and not simply to hide the assets for financial aid purposes. Some college advisors claim that any asset seen by the financial aid officer should be "hidden," because it will be used against you whether it "officially" counts in the financial aid formulas or not. These advisors are talking about cash value life insurance and annuities, neither of which is counted in the Federal financial aid calculation. However, these types of assets can be counted by private institutions. Generally the advice to hide an asset will come from someone in a position to get paid a commission if you move the money. Many traps are waiting for you when you re-position assets for financial aid purposes; therefore, you must get sound advice before proceeding.

The Free Application for Federal Student Aid (FAFSA)

Students and parents must complete the FAFSA form in order to receive any form of federal financial aid. The FAFSA cannot be filed until after January 1 of the student's senior year in high school and it must be filed each year the student is seeking financial aid. You can submit your FAFSA online at http://www.fafsa.ed.gov. Once a family submits the FAFSA form, the Department of Education's central processing system will calculate the EFC and report the results to both the colleges selected and the family. If you provided an email address when you applied for aid, you will receive your Student Aid Report (SAR) by email 3 to 5 days after your FAFSA has been processed. This email will contain a secure link to your SAR online. If you did not provide an email address when you applied, then you will receive a paper SAR by mail in 7 to 10 days after your FAFSA has been processed. If you do not receive the SAR report, you can call the federal processor at 1-800-4-FED-AID or you can write to:

Federal Student Aid Programs
P.O. Box 4038
Washington, DC 52243-4038

The SAR is a confusing government document that summarizes the information that you provided on the FAFSA. If there is an asterisk positioned next to the EFC figure on the SAR, then the data you submitted has been selected for verification (audit). The federal government requires that approximately 1/3 of FAFSA forms are sent for verification. It is a federal offense to give false information on the FAFSA. If you are selected for verification, you will be required to submit additional documentation such as copies of your tax returns, W-2s and 1099 forms. The audit is conducted directly through the college's financial aid officer. If you do not have an EFC number on your SAR, then more information may be needed from you to process your application. Once your SAR is accurate and complete, each school will send you an award letter.

The Award Letter

You will receive an award letter from each school your student applied to in March or April of their senior year. The award letter will have several components including the total cost of attendance, your family's EFC, and any need-based or merit-based grants, awards or scholarships. It should also list any loans, work study or other financial aid being offered. Some schools give you a complete list of their cost of attendance while others will simply list tuition, fees, room and board. You'll need to build your own spreadsheet so that you can make an accurate comparison of your actual out-of-pocket costs. Do not include loans in your analysis. Colleges consider loans financial aid but you should not. You will generally have until May 1 to make a decision and you have three choices when you respond to the award letter:

1. You can accept the award letter as is
2. You can accept parts of the award and reject others or
3. You can request a revised financial aid package.

If you have decided to try number three and are going to request additional financial aid, good luck. At this point you're behind the power curve and it will be difficult to get additional financial aid unless something substantial has changed in your finances. Financial aid officers are very reluctant to change a financial aid package unless something dramatic changed like you've lost your job, someone's died or you just found out that you only have six months to live. A lot is written encouraging families to negotiate a financial award package, however most families find out that their cries for more money fall on deaf ears. Why? It is simply a matter of supply and demand.

Unfortunately, at the present time, colleges are being bombarded with more applications from better qualified students than ever before in history. The real answer to getting a good financial aid award letter is to *pre*-negotiate your financial aid. What I mean by that is to make sure your student applies to the right colleges in the first place. If you have applied to a list of colleges that are both good academic fits and also good financial fits there should be no big surprises when you get the award letters. That means you need to do your homework well in advance before you make an application to know typically what that college is going to give, either in terms of merit-based aid or need-based aid for the type of student you are. Never rely on sticker price alone.

Have you received an attractive financial aid offer? The answer is: maybe. In order to determine if the offer is a good one, you will have to do some research into the amount and type of aid that the college typically offers. Next you will need to determine where your student fits in relation to the student attributes this institution is looking for. For example, does your student fall into the top 25% of desired incoming freshman, the bottom 25% or the middle of the pack. We use several sources for this type of information, including Wintergreen Orchard House's "College Admissions Data, Hyper-Handbook" which contains a plethora of data to help our students check their offers against past offers from each college.

In general, there are several financial strategies that <u>can</u> help you fund college expenses without raiding your retirement funds, savings or cash flow. They include:

- Financial Aid strategies – to position both the parents and student for grants, tuition discounts and endowment-based scholarships.
- Tax strategies – to increase your potential tax savings that can be converted to pay college costs.
- Cash flow strategies – to find potential areas of cash flow improvement in your investments, health care costs,

insurance costs, mortgage cost, and current living expenses, all which can be used to help offset college costs.

All these strategies will be covered in the next chapter and please keep in mind that not all strategies will apply to every family and in rare cases you may not be able to benefit from any of the strategies if you fail to plan ahead.

During May 2008, Gallup interviewed 684 college-bound students and another 720 parents of college students between the ages of 18 and 24. The primary goal of the study was to determine how families were actually paying the college bill. Please see Exhibit 3 below. What is immediately apparent and disturbing is that almost 40% of the bill is being financed by debt. Students and families are paying for 85% of their college costs and nearly half of these families are borrowing to cover these expenses. Parents are paying about one third of the total cost of attendance from income and savings, and are borrowing another 16%. Students are contributing one third of the cost, mostly by taking out loans, with friends and relatives chipping in an additional 3%. Now for the bad news: grants and scholarships (money that does not have to be repaid) accounted for only 15%.

Exhibit3

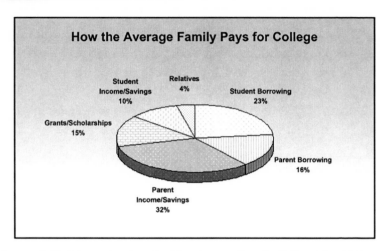

Source: Sallie Mae national study, *How America Pays for College*, May 2008 conducted by Gallup.

For example, higher income families paid substantially more for college and also paid more out of pocket expenses from their savings and income. Middle-income families borrowed more on average to pay for college than lower income families. Some of the most interesting results of the study were the values revealed by the respondents. 70% of students and parents said that potential post-graduation income of the student was not considered at all when making the decision to borrow money for college. This makes tremendous sense when you consider that 94% of the parents agreed with the statement that sending their child to college was an investment in their child's future. 96% of the students agreed on the same point. This agrees with what I currently see in my office as a college counselor. Most parents will state that they are willing to do "whatever it takes" when it comes to college. I could be wrong, but I would guess that most college CFOs were pretty happy to get that news.

You've Been Gapped

Each spring I get several calls from upset parents because they got gapped. Spring time is when families receive their financial award letters from each college they have applied to. It's called an award letter because it will show the total cost of attendance (COA) and any financial aid the college is awarding you. Remember, that "aid" can and generally will include loans. The difference between the total COA and the aid offered represents your out of pocket costs. The "award letter" is your bill. But what happens if the award letter shows you have need? A parent recently called about her son's award letter from a public university. Their family EFC was $15,000 per year and the annual cost of college was $22,700. Thus, they have a demonstrated need of $7,700 per year. The only aid offered by the college was a $3,500 student loan! They got gapped for $4,200 and will have to come out of pocket for this amount. In fact, they have actually received a tuition increase because the $3,500 loan will grow to $4,553.58 in four years, followed by $52.40 per month for 10 years to pay it off, for a total of $6,288.33. The $22,700 just grew to $25,488.33 for this student's freshman year only. The amazing thing is that colleges consider this giving you financial aid. Thank you very much.

Fewer than 4% of colleges meet 100% of families' need. The packaging of the award letter above is common and will generally consist of a combination of loans, work study and gapping (nothing). There are a small percentage of schools that meet 100% of need and will do so without offering loans. These are generally private colleges. Exactly what formula a particular college will use to determine how they will meet your need is shrouded in the mystery called Enrollment Management.

Most parents will never meet the university's enrollment manager, so let's take a quick look at college economics from the college's point of view. College enrollment management became prominent in the 90's when private colleges discovered that they were losing high-quality students to public universities due to "sticker price shock." Many private colleges were suffering from low admissions numbers and feared that they would go out of business if they did not find a better way to pinpoint those prospects most likely to attend their institution. To help with the problem, they turned to enrollment managers. An enrollment manager's goal is to shape the incoming freshman class and while doing so, to increase the net revenue per student. Fact: colleges are businesses. Fact: colleges would rather not admit that they are businesses. That's why you'll never meet the enrollment manager.

Here's how it works: first a private college hires an enrollment management firm (or hires a full time manager internally) to analyze the college's admissions policies, student enrollment patterns, demographics and diversity. The enrollment management firm analyzes the college's revenues and costs to determine the break-even point, or the number of students that the college needs to recruit and retain in order to cover their necessary expenses. The enrollment management firm then adds in the colleges projected new spending to determine the minimum revenue needed to achieve the college's total expenditure goals for the year. Now the enrollment management firm calculates the average expected family contribution per recruited student that is needed to meet the college's total expenditure goal. This is what the college calls their "target EFC." The enrollment management firm then develops a marketing campaign to target students of academic quality who live in the zip codes that will most likely yield the target EFC needed to meet the colleges' financial goals. The college will offer those students grants and scholarships equal to the difference between the college's total cost of tuition and the target EFC. Once the colleges recruit enough students to meet the break-even point, they will gradually begin to reduce the amount of grants and scholarships offered until the college is at full admissions.

The bottom line is that this process works. Some enrollment managers even predict how big a scholarship it will take to attract the kinds of students the college is short on, such as females for engineering schools and rural kids for urban colleges. In fact, enrollment management is so effective both private and public colleges are now using these techniques to minimize the amount of money they spend in order to meet their particular enrollment goals. I have greatly simplified the complex subject of enrollment management to illustrate what you are up against as a parent. Enrollment management has multiple purposes and is not specifically designed to hurt you – it simply is a widely utilized business technique that colleges use to plan and ultimately shape their incoming classes. Remember, colleges have a plan and you need one too.

Some Colleges Want to Share Your Financial Information

Prior to 1989, many colleges would regularly meet and share their financial aid policies with each other. The idea being that these meetings would allow them to adopt common policies that would focus on financially needy students. However, The US Justice Department saw this as an antitrust violation because these private colleges would meet and agree on common policies. Most of the colleges involved were the more elite, private colleges who were concerned about how they were spending their endowment money. These colleges would regularly examine the financial aid packages awarded to individual applicants who were admitted to multiple institutions. The idea was to make the offers comparable. If that's not the definition of collusion, I don't know what is. In 1989 this type of collaboration was deemed to be an illegal attempt to limit the size of financial aid packages. These colleges objected to the Justice Department's interpretation and have been crying big crocodile tears ever since.

According to Inside Higher Education, June 13, 2008 this issue has reared its ugly head again. Apparently most private college leaders and financial aid officers are upset that they are spending too much money on merit aid and not enough money on need-based aid. If you ask these college leaders why they simply don't shift more money to needy students, they complain that if they shift these funds to needy students, they will lose better, meritorious students to their competitors. As the theory goes, if they did lose their best students their SAT averages would drop and of course they would drop in the rankings according to U.S. News & World Report, etc., etc. I will let you decide for yourself but to me this is nothing more than a veiled attempt for private colleges to collude in an effort to preserve their mammoth endowment funds. It's outrageous. So apparently a group called the Institute for College Access and Success has put together a plan that urges Congress to create new exemptions to the existing antitrust law that would permit colleges to collaborate on financial aid policy. This is being pitched to Congress as a way to help poor students get more money. If colleges can offer less to the middle class, they'll have more to give to poor kids (the rich folks already pay full price). Unfortunately the real result would be price-fixing of merit based awards. What colleges don't like is that they have to compete for the best and brightest students by offering discounts. They would prefer to charge more. In other words, competition is causing colleges to charge less than if they didn't have to compete. The way that they can effectively eliminate the competition is to share your personal, financial, and academic information. The net effect is that it would allow them to keep more of their endowment funds in their own pocket at the public's expense. Competition drives prices down and they'd rather not compete. The bottom line is if this thing passes it will be bad news for both families and students.

Endowments

Imagine this for a moment: you dropped your child off at college two weeks ago and haven't heard a word. You're curious about how she's doing so you pick up the phone and give her a call. It's great to hear her voice, she loves college and all her classes except one are going great. You press her for a few more details and find out that her classes are being taught in a lecture hall with 300 to 400 other students! So naturally the question you have is what happens if your daughter has a question. She explains "No problem Dad". The lecture is complemented with a second class each week broken down into just 60 students. The smaller class is taught by a teaching assistant who is a graduate student at the college; so basically, your child is getting little or no contact with a full professor. When she has a question or needs further explanation, she is directed to the teaching assistant. At this point something very profound occurs to you. You paid full price for tuition, but your child isn't getting full access to a real professor. Instead she's being forced upon someone who generally has very little teaching experience and may only be a couple of years older than your daughter. Think about this carefully. As someone who's had the experience of a large public university where too many courses were taught in a lecture hall and also the experience of being taught by real professors with real Ph.D.'s in a class of only 6 students, I can tell you there is absolutely no comparison between the two.

Imagine now as you sip your morning coffee and scan your laptop for local news articles of interest, you notice that the president of the university where your daughter is attending is lamenting that the school's endowment has been hit hard during the recent downturn in the stock market. You're shocked to read that the endowment has lost over $200 million, but here's the real shocker. Even after the loss the endowment is still $1.3 billion! The president of the university is whining that they're going to have to cut back programs and students are going to be adversely affected because of the unfortunate losses of the school's endowment portfolio. In fact, the president will not receive a salary increase this year and will have to get by with her current pay of $1.3 million per year. At this point, you do what comes naturally and spit out a mouthful of coffee all over your computer screen. So think about it – the university president is whining because she can't increase her $1.3 million salary and the university's endowment lost $200 million. However, the endowment is still worth over $1 billion and your kid is sitting in class with over 300 of her best friends!

The example I just cited is fictitious and I'm sure you've heard the expression that the truth is sometimes stranger than fiction. For example, the president of Rensselaer Polytechnic Institute, Shirley Ann Jackson was criticized in a January 26, 2009 article of Inside Higher Education. The criticisms focused on Ms. Jackson's high salary and perks, in particular a second home in the Adirondacks (located on 36 acres of land) purchased by the university for $450,000. Ms. Jackson's salary is $1.3 million per year. Apparently her salary left her a little short because in addition to the second home, RPI was also providing an "executive housekeeper," as well as two separate "executive protection specialists" and an "executive protection coordinator." Evidently, when you make that kind of money you need extra security beyond just the campus police force. What is particularly disturbing about her salary and perks is that RPI had just laid off 80 employees as a cost-cutting measure.

It is my opinion that, in general, colleges are poorly run businesses. They are charging more and delivering less despite both increasing endowments and taxpayer subsidies. An independent policy group, the Delta Project on Postsecondary Education Costs, Productivity and Accountability found that between 2002 and 2006 tuition covered a larger share of the total cost, but that less money was being spent on classroom instruction. The report is based on data that colleges submit to the US Department of Education. The Delta Project analyzes the information and their report "Trends in College Spending: Where Does the Money Come From? Where Does It Go?" can be found on their website. These findings have some serious implications for lawmakers because according to Jane V. Wellman, executive director of the Delta Project, "we're packing a whole bunch of students into the institutions that spend the least per student." Remember, public universities are responsible for distributing federal monies in the form of Title IV funds as well as distributing state's tax dollars, both of which subsidize the cost. Even private colleges distribute federal Title IV funds in the form of student loans. I find it offensive that major universities are hoarding their endowments and at the same time raising tuition, cutting services and crying poor. Apparently, I'm not alone.

One industry critic is Bard College's president Leon Botstein and he has berated colleges for not spending more of the money raised through endowments. In a December 10, 2008 Inside Higher Education article, Botstein is quoted "Institutions should not be banks. They are not good at it, and they are no better than anybody else. It should come as no surprise that as investing vehicles, there was a certain amount of arrogance and hubris. There was much too much time and money spent on getting richer and richer without being clear about why." In a sentence, colleges have become poor money managers and they have consistently relied upon their endowments to subsidize poor decisions. According to Botstein, endowments should be used as a cash reserve against bad times as opposed to an offset for operating expenses. Essentially, these large institutions have become trust fund babies, but don't know how to run their household on their income. The minute the trust fund burps, everybody panics and announces cuts. Instead, colleges should be operating on their income. In order to do that effectively, you have to make sound professional decisions. For example,

Botstein plans to ask some of his professors to teach classes currently being taught by adjuncts. In other words, he's telling some of his faculty that they will have to teach the class themselves. In a second example, he is consolidating 15 separate courses into only two or three which will effectively teach the same material. He consistently looks for inefficiencies and smart ways to correct them. Sounds like basic management to me.

A recent Gallup poll found that students and parents are paying for approximately 85% of the college experience, and half of these families are forced to borrow money to do it. Grants and scholarships account for just 15% of the total outlay. The Gallup poll was part of a study titled "How America Pays for College," and surveyed 1,400 parents and students from around the country. They found that parents are paying about one third of the cost from their income and savings, and borrowing an additional 16%. Students are paying about one third of the cost predominantly by taking on debt. The report also showed that families earning less than $50,000 a year paid over $9,000 each year towards college expenses, while families earning between $50,000 and $100,000 paid on average $14,600 per year. Families earning more than $100,000 pay an average of $20,000 per year. No wonder college debt is skyrocketing. The hard fact is tuition increases have consistently outpaced inflation. Since 1992, inflation has averaged approximately 3% a year, however annual tuition increases have been double that. During this same time period, endowments have consistently continued to grow and in some cases they have grown fantastically. If you'd like to find out more about endowment size and growth, check out the National Association of College and University Business Officers website at www.NACUBO.org.

In recent months, some lawmakers have had their eye on endowments. In fact, it was recently proposed in Congress that universities spend a minimum of 5% of their endowment per year, which is the current requirement for charitable foundations. Presently, public institutions of higher learning on average only spend about 3 to 4% of their endowment per year. Most colleges oppose any law that would require them to payout more, and to date, nothing has changed. With all this negative publicity, I wasn't surprised to read the 2008 report "Trends in College Pricing" published by The College Board. According to their website, "The College Board is a not-for-profit membership association whose mission is to connect students to college success and opportunity. Founded in 1900, the association is composed of more than 5,400 schools, colleges, universities, and other educational organizations."

It is important to understand that The College Board represents the colleges. One of the main points of the report is that colleges are currently subsidizing approximately half of the real cost of tuition. Stop crying, because if colleges didn't subsidize the cost, you would actually have to pay double the tuition being charged now! If you look at this report a little more closely, you'll also find that the tuition at public universities over the last 10 years has grown at an inflation-adjusted 4.2%. To the casual reader, this may not sound like much, but if you run the numbers on that little 4.2%, the result is grotesque. Remember "inflation-adjusted" means that the 4.2% is in addition to inflation for 10 years. Said another way, your $80,000 public university four-year bachelor's degree would only cost $53,000 if the cost had only kept pace with inflation. The 4.2% adds $27,000 or an additional 51% to your costs. I think the College Board's Trends in College Pricing report from 2006 says it best. The report indicated that for a 25-year period from 1981 to 2006 real tuition prices (after adjusting for inflation) increased 150% at private, four-year institutions and almost 200% at public, four-year colleges and universities. The median household income for that same 25-year period grew at only 20% in real dollars.

Another outspoken critic on endowment hoarding is Lynne

Munson, an adjunct research fellow at the Center for College Affordability and Productivity. She also served as the deputy chairman for the National Endowment for the Humanities from 2001 until 2005. In an Inside Higher Education article, July 26, 2007 "Robbing the Rich to Give to the Richest," Lynn wrote "higher education endowments also are growing much faster than private foundations. The value of college and university endowments skyrocketed 17.7% last year, while private foundation assets increased 7.8%. Just 3.3% increase in academic endowments is attributable to new gifts. Most of the gain is a result of stingy and outdated endowment payout policies that retain and perpetually reinvest massive sums. This widespread practice results in a hoarding of tax-free funds." She further went on to state that university endowment spending averaged 4.2% while private foundations, although only required by law to spend 5%, actually spent on average 7%. Some universities have continued to grow their endowments, while families and students are being forced to take on ever-increasing debt to cover tuition increases. This is a serious issue when you consider that 66% of high school seniors go on to college.

It will be interesting to see if in the coming years Congress forces nonprofit colleges and universities to distribute more of their endowment funds for the public good. As the father of three, I can tell you that something has to give. Postsecondary education is a gigantic industry, but who is watching the store? I believe we need an independent auditing function of knowledgeable individuals to look at inefficiencies in these institutions to make sure taxpayer dollars are not wasted. Nonprofit colleges and universities enjoy tremendous tax benefits in near total autonomy. The result has been runaway tuition costs. A college education is no longer a luxury but rather a necessity if America is going to survive within this global economy. We cannot allow our institutions of higher learning to continue to place such an outrageous financial burden upon the public.

Colleges That Put Their Money Where Their Mouth Is

It is heartening to know that there are some colleges that believe a student should receive their bachelor's degree in four years and are willing to put their money where their mouth is. For example, as of December 2008, Manchester College in Indiana has announced a triple guarantee. First, students are assured enough financial aid to enroll, and second, if they cannot get the classes they need to graduate in four years, they pay no additional tuition for courses they take in the fifth year. Third, the college guarantees that within six months of graduation, students will either have a job or be admitted to graduate school. If this is not the case, the student is allowed to return the following year and take classes at no charge. There are some restrictions to receive the last part of the guarantee, including completing an internship, campus employment, and participating in at least one significant campus extracurricular activity or volunteer experience. Several other colleges also guarantee graduation in four years subject to certain restrictions. Basically, they allow any student who can't make it out in four years to continue taking classes at no charge. Below is a partial list of colleges that offer four-year graduation guarantees:

- University of the Pacific, Stockton California
- Regis University, Denver, Colorado
- Pace University, New York City
- Muskingum College, New Concord, Ohio
- Milwaukee School of Engineering, Milwaukee, Wisconsin
- Juniata College, Huntingdon, Pennsylvania
- Dominican University of California, San Rafael, California
- Doane College, Crete, Nebraska
- DePauw University, Greencastle, Indiana
- Centre College, Danfield, Kentucky

- Augsburg College, Minneapolis, Minnesota

I would like to see this type of guarantee extended to the public university system, especially since our public universities are funded in part with taxpayer dollars. There's absolutely no reason why a large public university or college cannot guarantee that a student will receive their bachelors degree within four years. There would of course need to be reasonable restrictions to receive the guarantee.

There are also several colleges where admission means a free ride. They include the United States Military Academy, West Point, New York; The United States Naval Academy in Annapolis, Maryland; The United States Coast Guard Academy in New London, Connecticut; The United States Air Force Academy, in Colorado Springs, Colorado; and The United States Merchant Marine Academy, in Great Neck, New York. Lesser-known free ride colleges also include Franklin W. Olin College of Engineering, Needham, Massachusetts; Cooper Union for the Advancement of Science and Art, New York City; and Deep Springs College, Deep Springs, California.

Another source for significantly reduced fees or free tuition is working colleges. Today there are only seven schools that meet the federal definition of a working college. All students who attend these colleges work on campus, farms or community centers, and most students work between 100 and 150 hours per semester. If you would like to learn more about working colleges you can visit their website at www.workcolleges.org. Some working colleges are listed below:

- Berea College, Berea Kentucky
- College of the Ozarks, Point Lookout, Missouri
- Alice Lloyd College, Pippa Passes, Kentucky
- Blackburn College, Carlinville, Illinois

- Ecclesia College, Springdale, Arkansas
- Sterling College, Craftsbury Common, Vermont
- Warren Wilson College, Asheville, North Carolina

Your Bottom Line

It is clear that the ultimate cost you pay for college is going to depend on many factors. Those factors include the college selected, how much debt you take on, the amount of financial aid, scholarships and grants you receive, and the time it takes to earn the degree. We have been brainwashed by the college industry into believing the notion that paying for college by any means necessary is required. This "debt for degree" mentality is growing. In a commentary by former Boston University vice president, Robert Ronstadt (The Chronicle of Higher Education, Feb. 27, 2009), states "The Project on Student Debt has found the amount of debt carried by graduates of four-year institutions has increased 60% in the past seven years. Average undergraduate-student debt was about $21,900 for those graduating in 2007. A fourth of those borrowing carried debts larger than $25,000. And, as alarming as those numbers are, they don't include money that parents have borrowed, or students' credit-card debt."

What you need to understand about college cost is this: you are at an extreme disadvantage unless you take control of those parts of the process that you <u>can</u> control. You cannot control whether or not a college decides to gap you or how much financial aid the government decides you deserve. Remember, the price you are asked to pay is discriminatory. Everyone pays a different price (even at the same college) and that price is only set *after* parents and students have disclosed their personal financial information. Imagine if the price of everything you need was determined this way. How would you feel if you were required to disclose your income and assets to the car salesman before he quotes the price of that new car?

The Right Fit™ Program is about controlling what you can, and what you absolutely can control is the fit. A good fit means a college with the right majors, less time to graduate, more free endowment-based scholarships and fewer loans. It is the best method to reduce your costs.

Chapter Five:
"reduce the cost of college"

The strategies outlined in this book may not be suitable for every individual, and are not guaranteed or warranted to produce any particular result. This book is sold with the understanding that neither publisher nor author, through this book, is engaged in rendering legal, tax, investment, insurance, financial, accounting, or other professional advice or services. If the reader requires such services, a competent professional should be consulted. Relevant laws, programs and policies vary from state to state.

Get Free Tuition and Actually Get Money Back

One popular method of decreasing the cost of college includes attending a 2-year college, receiving your associate's degree and then transferring to a four-year college to secure your bachelor's degree. This can be very effective in states like Florida that have strong articulation agreements between community colleges and the public university system; however, the key to making this strategy successful is to ensure that the student's ultimate goal is clear. The Right Fit™ Program helps all students meet their goals. The goal of this strategy is to show one method of using Federal tax credits when a student receives a merit scholarship and plans to attend a 2-year college first.

First let's do a quick review of the difference between tax credits and tax deductions. Tax credits are more powerful than tax deductions. A tax deduction only reduces the amount of your income by the deduction amount. So, if you make $80,000 and receive a tax deduction of $1,000, your income is reduced by the $1,000 deduction, and the tax savings equals $1,000 multiplied by your marginal tax bracket. Assuming your marginal tax bracket is 25%, then your tax bill is reduced by $1,000 X 25% = $250. A tax credit works much differently. Tax credits are a dollar for dollar reduction in your tax liability. For example, a $1,000 tax credit will reduce your tax bill by $1,000! That's four times more savings in your pocket compared to a deduction, so tax credits are very powerful. This example is an approximation only and many factors will determine the exact outcome.

Let's assume that while in high school your student earns a scholarship, for example the Academic Scholars award, and plans to attend a two year community college. Assume the Academic Scholars award is $1,326 per semester or $2,652 per year. Further, we'll assume the cost of the community college is $4,000 per year, which includes tuition and fees. If the student uses the $2,652 of scholarship funds to pay for tuition and fees and the parent's income is less than $160,000 (married filing jointly, tax year 2009) or $80,000 (single filer), the parents would qualify for only $548 using the American Opportunity Tax credit (the 2009 Recovery Act, to date the Presidents' 2010 budget would make this permanent). This is because, according to the IRS, you must reduce any qualified education expenses by the amount of scholarships before you calculate any possible tax credits. You can pick up a copy of IRS Publication 970 for all of the gory details.

However, instead of using the scholarship directly for tuition, suppose the family pays for tuition and fees with spendable income, a Stafford loan or the sale of investments, etc. In this case, the scholarship would be an overpayment and as such, refundable to the student. Further, assuming that the Academic Scholars award is a non-restrictive scholarship, it can be used to pay for either qualified or non-qualified college expenses. If the student elects to use the scholarship for nonqualified expenses, the student must complete a tax return and claim the scholarship as taxable income. In most cases, the student will not have to pay any taxes if the scholarship is less than the standard deduction ($5,700 in 2009).

When a family pays for a college education with sources not including the scholarship and concurrently receives a non-restrictive merit scholarship, they have over-paid the educational cost. If this occurs, the student can go to his or her college and get this over payment ($2,652) refunded. Since the family paid for the tuition and fees from an out-of-pocket source (income, loans, investments, etc.), the parents can then claim The American Opportunity Tax credit of up to $2,500. With the addition of the $2,652 scholarship and the $2,500 tax credit, the family now has a total of $5,152 of income. The family can then reimburse themselves for the money spent or pay off any loans taken out ($4,000 tuition and fees) and still have $1,152 left over! If the family were to do this over the next two years of the community college education, they would make a profit of $2,304. This extra money can be applied to the four year college when the student transfers after their sophomore year. The bottom line is that the family has paid for two years of community college and made an additional $2,304 of profit that they can spend any way they so choose. In conclusion, by knowing how scholarships and educational tax credits work together, families can reduce the cost of attending college by thousands of dollars.

529 Plans: Much Ado About Nothing

This may surprise you but I'm amazed at all the attention paid to 529 college savings plans. These plans were born in 1996 from federal legislation, and like all things that come from the government, these plans have many rules and regulations. In short, the money goes into these plans much easier than it comes out. To make matters worse, these plans are approved by each state with its own nuances and fee structures and some of those fee structures are grotesque. When money goes into these plans the federal government does not allow a tax deduction, however, there are a few states that do allow a tax deduction on their state income tax returns. In order to get this state income tax deduction, some states require that you invest in their particular 529 plan. Some states give a full or partial tax deduction no matter which 529 plan you choose. No matter how you look at it, whether or not you will receive a state income tax deduction, in my opinion is not worth worrying about. A lot is also made about the fee structure in many states 529 plans. A lot of authors spend an inordinate amount of time warning you about the high fee structure of some 529 plans. These arguments although factually correct, miss the bigger issue. For example, when I ask people (including accountants) if the earnings inside of 529 plans are tax-free, 9 out of 10 times, they answer yes. Unfortunately, this is the wrong answer. The correct answer is that distributed earnings of a 529 plan **may be tax-free**. The better questions to ask are:

1. How will a distribution from a 529 plan affect eligibility for financial aid?
2. How will the 529 plan affect merit-based financial aid?

A 529 plan is counted as a parental asset in the financial aid formulas. This means that the value of the plan is multiplied by 5.6% with the result added to your expected family contribution (EFC).

For example, if you have $80,000 in your child's 529 plan, 5.6% times $80,000 equals $4,480 that is added to the amount that you are expected to pay towards college each year. Or said another way, your eligibility for financial aid is reduced by $4,480 per year. The second question is a bit of a trick question, and a great way to tell if you're speaking to a knowledgeable college advisor. Merit-based financial aid is not dependent on your expected family contribution or for that matter your savings. In other words, merit-based financial aid is all about the merits of the student. So technically, assets in a 529 plan should not affect merit-based aid. However, most colleges will require you to disclose the value of 529 plan assets before they award the final amount of merit-based aid.

Put yourself in the financial aid officer's shoes for a moment. A bright student applies to your university; you want the student to attend, so you initially award a $5,000 per year presidential scholarship. You may do this without knowing any of the family's financials. You're willing to spend as much as $12,000 a year in endowment funds towards the student but before you add the additional $7,000 per year, you would like to see whether or not the family can afford your school. You require the family to submit either the FAFSA form (or the CSS Profile) and on those forms you see that the family has $80,000 in a college 529 plan. What would you do if you were the financial aid officer at this college? Would you take the $80,000, which is clearly an asset designed to be spent on college, and divide by four which equals $20,000 per year? Would you offer the student an additional $7,000 per year scholarship? Or would you assume that the student has $20,000 per year to spend towards college expenses?

Now suppose that same $80,000 was instead in the parent's IRA or another parental savings account. Do you think that a financial aid officer might be more inclined to multiply the $80,000 by 5.6% which equals $4,480? You might then make the following calculation $7,000 - $4,480 = $2,520 and offer this student an additional $2,520 per year in scholarship money. So the answer to the second question is a bit more complicated and the only person who can truly answer is the financial aid officer at that particular college. If the $80,000 is in a parental IRA, it may not be considered at all. Please see the next section "A Simple and Powerful Way to Use an IRA" on how you can still use those assets for college.

According to IRS publication 970, there are two types of plans: a prepaid plan and savings plan. These plans are established by the state in which you live and each state has at least one 529 plan. Contributions to a 529 plan are not tax-deductible on your federal income tax return but may have favorable income tax treatment in your home state. According to the IRS, distributions must be used to pay for qualified educational expenses. These expenses are tuition, fees, books, supplies, and required equipment for enrollment or attendance at an eligible educational institution. These expenses include reasonable costs for room and board for the beneficiary who is at least a part-time student. Let's address the question of whether or not distributions from a 529 college savings plan are indeed tax-free. Although I'll do my best to explain those details now, please refer to IRS publication 970 for your own edification.

Your original investment into a 529 college savings plan is not taxable upon distribution because you did not receive a tax deduction for the contribution. However, if you received a state income tax deduction for your original contributions you may owe state income tax upon distribution. This varies from state to state, so you'll have to check with your home state. 529 plan distributions are tax-free if the total distribution is less than or equal to adjusted qualified educational expenses. And you guessed it; the fun begins with the term adjusted qualified educational expenses. For example, when it comes to room and board, qualified expenses are only allowed to the extent that they are not more than the greater of the following two amounts:

- The allowance for room and board, as determined by the college or university, that was included in the cost of attendance (COA). This figure is the amount that is publicized in the college or university's documents.
- The actual amount charged if the student is residing in housing owned or operated by the college or university.

The 529 plan owner will receive Form 1099-Q for each plan distribution and you'll find in Box 1 the total amount of withdrawals and in Box 2 the amount of earnings. You should receive this form by January 31 of the year following the year a distribution was taken. The first thing you'll need to do is figure out the amount of your adjusted qualified expenses. Qualified expenses are tuition, fees, books, supplies, and required equipment (computers) for enrollment or attendance and room and board as described above. To determine adjusted qualified expenses, take your qualified expenses and subtract the following:

- The tax-free part of scholarships, grants and fellowships.
- Veterans educational assistance
- Pell grants
- Employer-provided educational assistance (section 127 plans)
- Any other non-taxable payments (other than gifts or inheritances) received as educational assistance.

Here is how to determine if tax is due:

1. Multiply the total distributed earnings shown on form

1099-Q. (Box 2) by the following fraction. The numerator of the fraction is the adjusted qualified education expenses paid during the year and the denominator is the total amount distributed during the year.

2. Subtract the amount calculated in step one above the total distributed earnings. This is the amount that must be included as taxable income.

$$\text{Distributed Earnings} \times \left(\frac{\text{Adjusted Qualified Expenses}}{\text{Total Amount Distributed}} \right)$$

Distributed Earnings – The results from the formula above = Taxable Earnings

For example, assume mom and dad invested a total of $15,000 into a 529 plan and over the years and the account grew to $25,000. Further, the first semester total qualified expenses equal $7,500. The student pays for these expenses with a $4,000 per semester scholarship and the parents withdraw $4,000 from the 529 plan. Part of the 529 distribution will be taxable as follows:

Total qualified expenses	$7,500
Tax-free scholarship	$4,000
Adjusted Qualified Expenses	$3,500

Now we have to apply the formula from above,

$1,600 (earnings) X $3,500 (adjusted qualified expenses)
$4,000 (distribution)
= $1,400 tax-free
$1,600 - $1,400 equals $200 taxable earnings.

This family will have to report a $200 taxable gain on their income tax return for their students' first semester, freshman year. It's important for you to understand that when you take a taxable distribution from a 529 plan, you will also incur a 10% penalty on the taxable portion of distribution. What a pain! For families that may qualify for The American Opportunity tax credit and who also have 529 college savings plans, a similar calculation has to be made. In this case, families cannot receive both a tax-free 529 plan distribution and a tax credit for the same expenses. In other words, your total qualified educational expenses must be reduced by any expenses taken into account when figuring The American Opportunity Tax credit. You can see examples of how to make that calculation in IRS publication 970.

Assets in 529 plans can be rolled over or transferred from one plan to another. Additionally, you can change the beneficiary without transferring the account assets. A couple other important points to note are that the 529 plan can be owned by a student. Generally this can happen when assets are sold in an UGMA/UTMA account and put into the 529 plan. In this case, even though the student legally owns the assets, they are counted as an asset of the parents on the FAFSA and assessed at the 5.6% rate.

So, are 529 plans a good idea? If the family is in a very high tax bracket and is absolutely certain that they will not qualify for any federal financial aid or merit-based aid, and they begin when the child is young, then 529 plans are probably acceptable savings vehicles for college. The problem is when you start putting money into a 529 plan you probably won't have a very accurate estimate of what type of aid you might be eligible for, especially merit-based aid. The bottom line is that these types of programs, like all government programs, come with a lot of strings attached. It's been my experience for the vast majority of families that have 529 plans; the actual tax savings they receive are very modest. To me, it's much simpler to save in a separate account under the parents' name. If the parents have the discipline to put money into a 529 plan, they generally have the discipline to not touch the college fund.

A Simple and Powerful Way to Use an IRA

Here is a great way to use an IRA for college without paying taxes or penalties once you have made the careful decision to fund all or a part of college expenses by taking distributions from an IRA. First we will review a few IRA basics and then I will illustrate this strategy by showing you how we helped one family use an IRA to supplement college *without* destroying the account.

Let's review the penalty-free, early withdrawal rule first. According to the IRS, a distribution from an IRA prior to age 59½ will be subject to a 10% early withdrawal penalty. However, the IRS allows an exception to the 10% penalty if the withdrawal is used to pay for undergraduate or graduate qualified education expenses. The money must be spent on the taxpayer, the taxpayer's spouse, child or grandchild and be paid to an eligible educational institution. This has been the case for distributions made after December 31, 1997. The penalty-free withdrawal is only available if used to pay for "qualified education expenses." The IRS changes the definition of "qualified education expense" depending on the subject at hand. For example, when considering the use of tax credits, room and board *is not* a qualified education expense. But when considering penalty-free distributions from an IRA, room and board *is* a qualified education expense. This is a critical difference as you will see in the example to follow. If you would like to read all the details, please get a copy of IRS Publication, 590, "Individual Retirement Arrangements (IRAs)."

Another point to know is that any tax-free distributions from a Coverdale Educational Savings Account, U.S. Savings Bond, 529 Tuition Savings Plan, Prepaid Plan, or employer-provided educational assistance plan will reduce the amount of qualified expenses dollar for dollar that can be used for the penalty-free IRA distribution. All these details can be found in IRS Publication 970, "Tax Benefits for Education." So the good news is that you can use the money for college and not pay the penalty, but you still owe taxes on the distribution. This can be a problem for some families that would otherwise qualify for federal financial aid, because the amount withdrawn is considered income and will increase the adjusted gross income (AGI) on their tax return by the amount of the IRA withdrawal. This in turn can cause the loss of Federal Aid by as much as 47% of the increase in AGI. For example, if a family takes $10,000 out of an IRA, they could lose as much as $4,700 in aid. If the family is not eligible for Federal Aid, and most are not, then this will not be an issue. The point is that any significant distribution from an IRA will cause a nasty tax bill and a possible reduction in financial aid. This is despite the fact that the money will not be penalized when properly used for college. This is where most information ends on the subject of using IRA money for college – although you get to avoid the 10% penalty, you still get to enjoy the tax bill! In the example below, we go much deeper into the IRA rules and show you a case where we used a different "penalty-free rule" to greater advantage.

IRS section 72(t) allows penalty-free distributions (prior to age 59½) from IRAs under one of three different distribution methods. These rules have nothing to do with college; they are just methods to avoid the 10% early withdrawal penalty. Like most of the IRS rules and regulations, they are somewhat complicated but a competent College Counselor, CPA or CFP can easily set this type of plan up for you. As long as you follow the guidelines, you are allowed (before age 59½) to take ***substantially equal periodic*** payments from an IRA without penalty.

Case Study: Calvin Is Short $50,000 for College

Here is the situation that Calvin found himself in: his Dad had both saved and paid for Calvin's first four years of college, but Calvin found himself needing an additional 1-2 years in order to graduate with the degree he would need to land a good job in his field. Please don't be surprised by this situation because, according to The National Center for Education Statistics, 2 out of 3 students have NOT graduated in four years.

Calvin was already maxed-out on student loans and his dad was not comfortable co-signing for any high interest rate private loans. Dad did not have any excess monthly cash flow to fund the extra years. However, Dad did have a $100,000 IRA (in addition to other retirement plans and savings) that he was willing to dip into for the additional $50,000. Calvin has a nice dad. Further, Dad was aware that he could take distributions from the IRA without penalty. Also, the family was not eligible for Federal Aid, so no loss of financial aid would result from the additional income. His question to me was: Is there a better way to use the IRA than simply taking out the $50,000 over the next two years and paying all those income taxes? Here is what we did:

The first option was to simply take out about $69,400, pay approximately $19,400 in income taxes (28% tax bracket) and use the net $50,000 for college. There would be no penalties due. This would result in $30,600 remaining in Dad's IRA and assuming 7% growth for the next 15 years, Dad (age 45 today) would have an $84,426 balance at age 60. This option seemed fine to Calvin, but his Dad wasn't too happy with the IRA being worth less 15 years from now!

We recommended Dad consider a second option:

1. Take a $50,000, 15-year home equity loan at 5.75%

interest. Payments equal about $4,982 per year.

2. Use the $50,000 proceeds from the home loan to pay for the next two years of college.

3. Use the IRS special 72(t) rules to take about $4982 per year from the $100,000 IRA.

4. Pay the loan payments with the IRA distributions. This is a cash flow wash.

Additionally, assuming that the mortgage interest is fully deductable, the taxable IRA distributions are partially offset by the loan interest deduction and allow dad to spread the tax bill out over fifteen years instead of two. Also, because of 72(t), there are no penalties. This saves approximately $5,400 in taxes as follows:

15 years X $4,982 = $74,730 taxable IRA distributions - $24,737
interest deductions
= $49,993 X 28%
= $13,998 taxes paid

Versus

2 years X $34,700 = $69,400 taxable IRA distributions
= $19,432 taxes paid

The difference is $19,432
-$13,998
$5,434 in tax savings

The Results

Option one left Dad with about $84,426 in his IRA at age 60 and his son with the right degree. Option two left Dad with about $150,710 in his IRA at age 60 and his son with the right degree.

Option two assumes a 7% return and $4,982 withdrawals from the IRA for 15 years, beginning at the end of each year. The reason Dad has more in the IRA at age 60 under option two is because a much larger sum was allowed to compound over the 15 years – this is one of the biggest keys to money management. **Both strategies can be accomplished without penalties but option two leaves Dad with $66,000 more in his IRA at retirement and an additional $5,434 in tax savings.**

The critical thing to remember is that once the funds are removed under option one, it is too late to fix the mistake. Please make sure you know all your options before you launch into a plan that could cost you big money. College is already expensive as it is!

How to Pay for 60% to 80% of College Costs Using Just Your Current Income

According to "Trends in College Pricing 2008" released by College Board, the total estimated cost for public, four-year, in-state, on-campus students is $18,326 per year. These costs include tuition fees, room and board, books and supplies, transportation and other expenses. Below is an example from a family who visited with me in my office in Tampa, Florida. They're a family of four with children ages 18 and 14. Although neither parent has a college degree, their son works hard in high school, is motivated, and does have the grades to be accepted into a public university. Unfortunately, the parents simply haven't saved any money for college. The parents are very hard-working people and believe that their son should bear some of the cost burden for college. Here's their situation:

Student

- GPA equals 3.2, took one AP course and scored a two on the exam.

- Received 980 on the SAT I, and 23 on the ACT.
- Student has been accepted at a Florida public university.
- Total cost of attendance equals $18,000 per year.

Family Situation

- Family of four, children ages 18 and 14.
- Expected Family Contribution (EFC) equals $18,000 per year.
- Family adjusted gross income equals $96,000 per year, both parents work.
- Both parents save 6% into their 401(k) plans; this is their only regular savings.
- They believe if they cut back on extras, they could put $200 per month toward college.

The first step was to have the family put together a detailed budget so that we could determine exactly where they were spending their money each month. Despite the parents' best intentions and after review of their actual expenditures each month, we agreed upon $100 per month as the amount they actually will put toward college. We also agreed that their son would apply for and accept a government guaranteed Stafford loan of $5,500 for his freshman year. The budget analysis revealed the following:

- Average monthly food consumption per family member equals $200.
- Money spent on high school activities and events equals $100 per month.
- $100 per month is spent on gas and auto expenses, the student will not be taking a car to college.

For this family, there is approximately $400 per month that will be transferred to college. Additionally, a review of the family's tax return shows that they should qualify for The American Opportunity Tax credit of $2,500. So now let's put everything together.

Resources available for college:

- $400 per month in transferred expenses equals $4,800.
- $100 per month from the parent's income equals $1,200.
- Government-backed student Stafford loan equals $5,500.
- Federal tax credit equals $2,500.

The total funds available equal $14,000 which is 78% of the $18,000 per year cost of attendance. In other words, the family has 78% of the cost of college already covered with existing cash flow, a student loan, and tax credits. This still leaves the family short $4,000 a year. The good news for this student is that he lives in Florida which provides a state-wide merit scholarship program called the Bright Futures scholarship. Minimum requirements are a high school 3.0 GPA and 970 SAT score which this student has achieved. This will give the young man an additional $3,000 per year in scholarship funds from the state of Florida. Now the family has $17,000 covered or approximately 94% of the total cost and is only short $1,000 per year. At this point, the student has the option to either work during the summer or to accept a work study program at the University to cover the remaining $1,000 per year balance. If this family were to live in a state that does not have merit based scholarships like Florida's Bright Futures scholarship, the student would have to make up $4,000 per year via work study, a summer job, or both. Of course, the ultimate last resort to make up the $4,000 shortfall is for mom and dad to take parent loans of $4,000 per year. The moral of the story is that families of modest means can usually find a way to use existing cash-flow for college. It does require that they do their homework and know their family budget.

A Simple Cash Flow Strategy

Sometimes funding college is as simple as rearranging your existing cash flows. This is generally most effective if you have some debt and ultimately will involve consolidating those liabilities. Like all financial strategies, debt consolidation has pros and cons. Generally speaking debt consolidation does not reduce your debts it simply rearranges them in such a manner as to produce an improved cash flow. This means that you're spending less each month while paying interest for the privilege of using someone else's money; this can be more efficient from a cash flow standpoint. And college is a cash flow problem. You then use the extra cash flow to help pay the cost of college. Let's take a look at an example of a typical family, the Patel family, who would like to send their son to college but didn't know how they were going to pay for it. The Patel family has two children their oldest son Raja is a senior in high school and their youngest, Kelsey is a high school sophomore. Their total family income is $100,000 per year and unfortunately they've saved absolutely nothing towards Raja or Kelsey's college education. The first step is to scrub their budget and look for any areas where there could be some potential savings. Unfortunately for the Patel's, we were not able to find any additional monthly cash flow to put towards college. In fact the parents are only saving a modest 3% of their income into their 401(k) plans. They were however both very motivated to send their children to college and also did not want their children to graduate with any significant amount of debt. The parents were depressed because they had no idea how they could afford college.

Here's a snapshot of their financial situation:

Home value = $350,000

Current Liabilities:		
Type	**Balance**	**Monthly Payment**
Primary Mortgage Balance	$72,582	$750
Car Loan #1	$4,389	$286
Car Loan #2	$12,717	$500
Other Consumer Loan	$19,833	$290
2nd Mortgage	$17,400	$500
Total Liabilities:	**$126,921**	
Total Monthly Payments:	**$2,326**	

The decision was made to obtain a new mortgage at 80% loan to value, using a conventional 30-year fixed at 6.0% interest. This resulted in:

Total Mortgage:	**$280,000**
- Total Debt Paid Off:	$126,921
- Loan Costs / Fees:	$5,000
Total Savings:	**$148,079**

This resulted in a new single monthly payment of $1,679

Old monthly payment = $2,326

Improved monthly cash flow = $647

Additional monthly tax savings +$200

Total Positive Monthly Cash Flow = **$847**

Additionally, they now have a lump sum of $148,079 in their pocket. This will provide approximately $70,000 a piece for the two kid's college, and leave them with $8,079 to use as an emergency fund. The additional monthly tax savings are a result of the larger mortgage being tax-deductible on Schedule A of their 1040 tax return. Any benefit from this tax deduction will depend on both the particular financial situation of the family and the Internal Revenue Code. Of course, the family now also has a $280,000 mortgage which represents $148,000 more debt than previously. Every family gets to a make a choice. For this family, they were clear about wanting to send their kids to college if at all possible. They were also clear that they did not want their children to take debt to do so. Lastly, this family was very concerned about paying off their home prior to retirement so my recommendation was for them to apply the extra cash flow of $847 per month towards their new mortgage to pay it off early. Making this payment each month will have the new mortgage paid off in approximately $13^{1/2}$ years, well before they retire. In summary, the lump sum pays for college and the monthly cash flow pays off the debt. This plan is only as good as the family's commitment to religiously pay their debt down with the additional cash flow. If they fail to do this, all they have done is increase their debt (because of the college costs), but they were going to do that anyway.

Make Your Student the Bank

Here is a very simple idea. Assume that you will not qualify for financial aid because your income is too high. That's the bad news, but the good news is you have saved $50,000 in a trust account for your student. This will be a UTMA/UGMA account and now that your child is 18 years old, the money belongs to her. She has solid grades but not the kind of grades that lead to big scholarships at private colleges. You have read my book and realize that the odds are your daughter will be attending State U. for the better part of six years and you estimate that you will need closer to $70,000 from the trust account. The balance of the costs will be covered by summer jobs and modest student loans. Here's the plan: have your daughter cash in the trust assets and make a loan to you of the cash. You can make this a home equity loan or even a second mortgage. You can easily have the note drawn up by a sharp CPA or an attorney. Also, make sure you discuss the new Kiddie Tax rules so there are no surprises. You must ensure that the interest rate is reasonable. Pay your kid the interest and principal over the six years (total payments = approximately $70,000) and deduct the interest as an itemized deduction. I have seen this save families thousands in taxes on money that you were going to pay for college anyway. If for some reason you need to give your student more of the funds sooner, simply accelerate the loan payoff.

Final Thoughts

Do You Need a Professional College Counselor?

Sometimes the most expensive advice you will receive is free. Too often families focus on the short term costs and miss out on the long term savings. Most families somehow manage to get through the college process either on their own or with the help of high school guidance counselors. Most families find a way to pay for college using a combination of loans, income, and savings. However, there are situations where hiring an experienced professional college counselor is a better idea.

Although most guidance counselors today are both hard-working and committed to helping students, they are also burdened with too many students and not enough hours in the day. If you are lucky enough to be able to afford a top, private high school, this may be no issue at all. However, it is unlikely that your student is receiving anything approaching The Right Fit™ Program for college. This is especially true when considering career counseling and personal finance strategies. Most high school-level counselors are simply not trained or equipped to advise families on financial matters related to college. Additionally, there is a prevailing misconception that career counseling should begin in college. The better solution is to begin career counseling in high school and *continue* it in college. Some of the common complaints we often hear are:

- The guidance counselor knows little about how to apply to very selective colleges
- The guidance counselor only knows about in-state colleges
- The guidance counselor doesn't know my child
- The guidance counselor has hundreds of students assigned to him/her.
- The guidance counselor is new or seems over-whelmed
- The guidance counselor is focused on the "problem" kids

College is very serious business, and you can be guaranteed that on the other side of the process is a professional whose loyalties lie with the college.

You may want to use a professional if you are having difficulty developing a complete list of candidate colleges. The college search process can be daunting and is often a source of tension between students and parents. With thousands of colleges to choose from, it is more than understandable that building this critical list gets confusing and frustrating. Tragically, too many families give up and in the end, make a poor choice. The transfer and four-year graduation statistics bear this out. A pro can be a big help by using proven methodologies and experience. The result is a solid, focused college search that produces a good fit for both the student's academic record and the family's finances.

Professional counseling can also be of tremendous benefit if the student's strongest attributes are not the SAT/ACT scores or GPA. Some public universities today are turning away students that would have easily been admitted just a few years ago. This is hard on kids. Don't worry. There are many good schools where the "numbers" are not the first priority. The right person can help with student essays, recommendations, and other information to increase your students' probability of admission.

The most important lesson I can leave you with is this: take the time to identify and match your student with the right fit career. Go systematically step by step through the Right Fit™ Program, while thoroughly understanding all of the financial and bureaucratic implications attached to the college admissions process, so you and your family can make educated decisions about the future life path of your student. Although the college process is a very complicated maze to make your way through, this book provides you with a solid foundation to get started. There are also several additional free resources on my website: www.kennethalbert.com. If you get stuck, or if you're in doubt, don't hesitate in getting professional help. It could save you thousands!

Appendix A

National Survey of Student Engagement

Benchmarks of Effective Educational Practice

Level of Academic Challenge
Challenging intellectual and creative work is central to student learning in collegiate quality. Colleges and universities promote high levels of student achievement by emphasizing the importance of academic effort in setting high expectations for student performance.

Activities and conditions:

- Time spent preparing for class (studying, reading, writing, rehearsing, and other activities related to your academic program)
- Work harder than you thought you could to meet an instructor's standards or expectations
- Number of assigned textbooks, books or book length packs of course readings
- Number of written papers or reports of 20 pages or more

- Number of written papers or reports between five and 19 pages
- Number of written papers or reports fewer than five pages
- Coursework emphasizes: analyzing the basic elements of an idea, experience, or theory
- Coursework emphasizes: synthesizing and organizing ideas, information, or experiences
- Coursework emphasizes: making adjustments about the value of information, arguments, or methods
- Coursework emphasizes: applying theories or concepts to practical problems or in new situations
- Campus environment emphasizes spending significant amounts of time studying and on academic work

Active and Collaborative Learning

Students learn more when they are intensely involved in education and are asked to think about and apply what they are learning in different settings. Collaborating with others in solving problems or mastering difficult material prepares students to deal with the messy, unscripted problems that they will encounter daily during and after college.

Activities:

- Asked questions in class or contributed to class discussions
- Made a class presentation
- Work with other students on projects during class
- Work with classmates outside of class to prepare class assignments
- Tutored or taught other students
- Participated in a community-based project as part of a regular course

- Discussed ideas from readings or classes with others outside of class (students, family members, coworkers, etc.)

Student-Faculty Interaction

Students see firsthand how experts think about and solve practical problems by interacting with faculty members inside and outside the classroom. As a result, their teachers become role models, mentors, and guides for continuous, lifelong learning.

Activities:

- Discussed grades and assignments with an instructor
- Talked about their career plans with a faculty member or advisor
- Discussed ideas from their readings or classes with faculty members outside the class
- Worked with faculty members on activities other than coursework (committees, orientation, student life activities, etc.)
- Received prompt written or oral feedback from faculty on your academic performance
- Worked with a faculty member on a research project

Supportive Campus Environment

Students perform better and are more satisfied at colleges that are committed to their success and cultivate positive working and social relations among different groups on campus.

Conditions:

- Campus environment provides support you need to help you succeed academically

- Campus environment helps you cope with your non-academic responsibilities (work, family, etc.)
- Campus environment provides the support you need to thrive socially
- Quality of relationships with other students
- Quality of relationships with faculty members
- Quality of relationships with administrative personnel and offices

Enriching Educational Experiences

Complimentary learning opportunities inside and outside the classroom augment the academic program. Experiencing diversity teaches students valuable things about themselves and other cultures. Used appropriately, technology facilitates learning and promotes collaboration between peers and instructors. Internships, community service, and senior capstone courses provide students with the opportunities to synthesize, integrate, and apply their knowledge. Such experiences make learning more meaningful and, ultimately, more useful because what students know becomes a part of who they are.

Activities and conditions:

- Talking with students with different religious beliefs, political opinions, or values
- Talking with students of a different race or ethnicity
- An institutional climate that encourages contact among students from different economic, social, and racial or ethnic backgrounds
- Using electronic technology to discuss or complete assignments

Participating in:

- Internships or field experiences
- Community service or volunteer work
- Foreign-language coursework
- Study abroad
- Independent study or self assigned major
- Culminating senior experience
- Co-curricular activities
- Learning communities

Appendix B

(Source: U.S. Department of Education's National Center for Educational Statistics)

Graduation Rate Data

The institutional graduation-rate data presented in College Results Online is collected by U.S. Department of Education's National Center for Education Statistics, through a centralized higher education data collection process called the Integrated Post-secondary Education Data System (IPEDS). IPEDS consists of a series of surveys through which institutions provide data about themselves on a variety of topics. One of those surveys is the Graduation Rate Survey (GRS).

The GRS graduation rates displayed on College Results Online are based on the percentage of first-time, full-time, bachelor's or equivalent degree-seeking freshmen who earn a bachelor's or equivalent degree from the institution where they originally enrolled. Undergraduates who begin as part-time or non bachelor's degree-seeking students, or who transfer into the institution from elsewhere in higher education, are not included in the GRS cohort. Their success or failure to earn a degree does not influence the GRS graduation rates in College Results Online in any way.

In addition to limiting the GRS cohort to those students described above, institutions are also allowed to exclude from their calculations any students who fail to earn a degree for the following reasons:

- Left school to serve in the armed forces.
- Left school to serve with a foreign aid service of the federal government.
- Left school to serve on an official church mission.
- Died or became permanently disabled.

The GRS also collects the percentage of students who have transferred to another institution, and the percentage who have not graduated but are still enrolled in degree programs that take longer than four years to complete.

The latest survey form submitted by institutions for GRS data can be found here: http://nces.ed.gov/ipeds/pdf/webbase2004/grs_4yr_form.pdf. It's important to note that College Results Online does not include *every* 4-year Title-IV eligible higher education institution in the United States. It only contains institutions that meet all of the following criteria:

- They fall in the public or private not-for-profit sector. This excludes for-profit 4-year institutions like the University of Phoenix.
- They reported GRS data for the 2006 cohort.
- They were assigned a selectivity rating in Barron's *Profiles of American Colleges* 2007 Edition.

These restrictions limit the universe of 4-year institutions being analyzed to approximately 1,450 institutions. Accordingly, the results of statistical analyses and descriptions of this universe of institutions may vary from the results of corresponding descriptions of all 4-year institutions. However, because the institutions covered in that universe enrolled 96% of all students in the total 4-year non-profit bachelor's degree seeking GRS cohort, such variance is likely to be small.

Retention – Progression
4-Year, 5-Year, and 6-Year Graduation Rates:
These rates are cumulative. For example, the five-year graduation rate shows the percent of students who graduated in 5 years or *less*, not the percent who took exactly 5 years to graduate. (IPEDS)

Sector:
There are a number of different sectors of higher education, based on both length of academic programs (4-year, 2-year, less than 2-year), and financial status (public, private non-profit, private for-profit). College Results Online only contains data for 4-year institutions that are either public or private non-profit. The latter designation is abbreviated as "private." (IPEDS)

SAT and ACT Detail

Estimated Median SAT/ACT: Higher education institutions don't report median aggregate SAT or ACT data to IPEDS. For the SAT, they report the 25th and 75th percentile score of students submitting scores, for both the verbal and mathematics sections. For the ACT, they report the 25th and 75th percentile scores for the English, math, and composite scores.

The median composite ACT score is estimated by averaging the 25th percentile and 75th percentile composite ACT scores. The median combined SAT score is estimated by adding the average of the 25th and 75th percentile verbal score to the average of the 25th and 75th percentile math score, and dividing by two.

Some institutions accept only the SAT or the ACT, while some accept both. For institutions that only accept the ACT, the estimated median ACT score was converted to an SAT equivalent using a concordance table based on a study of students who take both exams. (Neil Dorans, C. Felicia Lyu, Mary Pommerich and Walter Houston, "Concordance Between ACT Assessment and Recentered SAT I Sum Scores" *College and University* 73 (2) pg. 24-35.)

The 25th and 75th percentile composite ACT scores were converted, and then averaged. For institutions accepting both tests, either the SAT or converted ACT score was used, depending on which test made up the majority of all test scores submitted by first-time first-year degree-seeking freshmen. (IPEDS)

Outside sources were used to confirm the validity of the SAT data reported to IPEDS. In certain cases where there were tremendous inconsistencies in the IPEDS SAT data, SAT values from outside sources were substituted.

Finance, Financial Aid, and Faculty

Student and Related Expenditures/FTE: This is an intermediate financial measure, including instructional, student services, and academic support expenditures. The specific formula was developed by the National Center for Higher Education Management Systems (NCHEMS). Student-related expenditures are calculated as (Instruction + Student Services + Academic Support*(Instruction / (Instruction + Public Service + Research))). (IPEDS)

Name	4yr Grad Rate	State	Median SAT	Size	Sector	Student Related Exp./FTE
Amherst College	88%	MA	1,455	1,612	Private	$34,685
Art Center College of Design	73%	CA	N/A	1,367	Private	$32,496
Augustana College - Illinois	73%	IL	1,205	2,371	Private	$14,936
Austin College	72%	TX	1,255	1,290	Private	$15,946
Allegheny College	70%	PA	1,230	2,024	Private	$17,842
Assumption College	69%	MA	1,075	2,226	Private	$12,006
Albion College	67%	MI	1,125	1,954	Private	$15,035
American University	64%	DC	1,270	5,723	Private	$17,898
Alma College	58%	MI	1,085	1,257	Private	$14,279
Albany College of Pharmacy	56%	NY	1,160	864	Private	$13,336
Albertson College of Idaho	55%	ID	1,065	774	Private	$12,786
Asbury College	55%	KY	1,145	1,160	Private	$13,050
Anna Maria College	54%	MA	925	608	Private	$8,673
Allen College	52%	IA	990	337	Private	$5,098
Adelphi University	51%	NY	1,110	4,227	Private	$14,122
Albright College	51%	PA	1,040	2,081	Private	$11,553
Arcadia University	50%	PA	1,080	1,819	Private	$13,875
Alfred University	49%	NY	1,125	1,896	Private	$17,932
Augustana College - South Dakota	48%	SD	1,190	1,652	Private	$10,516
American International College	47%	MA	977	1,275	Private	$10,261
Azusa Pacific University	47%	CA	1,115	4,165	Private	$15,083
Ashland University	42%	OH	1,045	2,604	Private	$8,499
Anderson University	39%	IN	1,055	2,212	Private	$12,217
Albertus Magnus College	38%	CT	953	1,724	Private	$4,695
Art Academy of Cincinnati	38%	OH	990	161	Private	$17,333
Abilene Christian University	35%	TX	1,117	3,993	Private	$8,188
Aurora University	35%	IL	990	1,760	Private	$9,907
Appalachian State University	34%	NC	1,125	12,357	Public	$7,857
Auburn University Main Campus	33%	AL	1,105	18,270	Public	$9,544
Augsburg College	32%	MN	1,045	2,429	Private	$12,155
Andrews University	32%	MI	1,045	1,568	Private	$16,811
Alice Lloyd College	30%	KY	970	620	Private	$6,185
Alderson Broaddus College	30%	WV	1,010	611	Private	$11,197
Alvernia College	30%	PA	955	1,675	Private	$9,321
Antioch College	29%	OH	N/A	453	Private	N/A
Arizona State University at the Tempe Campus	28%	AZ	1,110	35,662	Public	$10,164

Name	4yr Grad Rate	State	Median SAT	Size	Sector	Student Related Exp./FTE
Atlantic Union College	27%	MA	830	420	Private	$14,582
Adrian College	26%	MI	990	947	Private	$10,981
Aquinas College - Michigan	25%	MI	1,025	1,573	Private	$8,892
Averett University	23%	VA	979	1,434	Private	$8,397
Avila University	22%	MO	1,010	1,011	Private	$8,185
Alcorn State University	22%	MS	845	2,771	Public	$8,525
Alaska Pacific University	21%	AK	1,015	418	Private	$15,283
Arkansas State University- Main Campus	19%	AR	990	7,842	Public	$6,571
Arkansas Tech University	18%	AR	1,025	5,686	Public	$4,976
Alverno College	17%	WI	930	1,735	Private	$10,599
Angelo State University	17%	TX	950	5,130	Public	$6,516
Alabama State University	15%	AL	745	4,134	Public	$7,461
Aquinas College - Tennessee	14%	TN	1,000	503	Private	$7,788
Adams State College	14%	CO	930	2,136	Public	$4,114
Albany State University	12%	GA	925	2,875	Public	$8,905
Auburn University- Montgomery	12%	AL	970	3,235	Public	$7,659
Austin Peay State University	12%	TN	990	6,971	Public	$6,696
Alabama A & M University	12%	AL	865	4,770	Public	$6,548
Augusta State University	6%	GA	970	4,278	Public	$6,026
Armstrong Atlantic State University	5%	GA	1,035	4,416	Public	$6,898
American Indian College of the Assemblies of God Inc	N/A	AZ	N/A	59	Private	$13,734
Arkansas Baptist College	N/A	AR	N/A	268	Private	$4,476
Agnes Scott College	N/A	GA	1,223	920	Private	$23,734
Atlanta College of Art	N/A	GA	990	305	Private	$15,487
Allen University	N/A	SC	N/A	609	Private	$7,023
Boston College	88%	MA	1,335	9,694	Private	$20,221
Bates College	86%	ME	1,355	1,699	Private	$28,269
Babson College	86%	MA	1,250	1,725	Private	$26,652
Bucknell University	85%	PA	1,310	3,579	Private	$24,822
Bowdoin College	84%	ME	1,395	1,663	Private	$36,162
Brandeis University	83%	MA	1,350	3,250	Private	$23,812
Brown University	83%	RI	1,435	6,013	Private	$31,170
Beacon College ()	77%	FL	N/A	99	Private	$10,754
Beacon College (FL)	77%	FL	N/A	99	Private	$10,754
Bentley College	73%	MA	1,225	4,120	Private	$17,916
Boston University	70%	MA	1,300	17,821	Private	$27,150
Bard College	62%	NY	N/A	1,818	Private	$23,474
Bethel University	62%	MN	1,145	2,982	Private	$11,859
Bryant University	62%	RI	1,115	3,076	Private	$14,411

Name	4yr Grad Rate	State	Median SAT	Size	Sector	Student Related Exp./FTE
Birmingham Southern College	60%	AL	1,185	1,304	Private	$20,951
Bridgewater College	60%	VA	1,055	1,499	Private	$11,635
Butler University	59%	IN	1,180	3,601	Private	$13,575
Bethany College - West Virginia	58%	WV	985	896	Private	$9,919
Beloit College	55%	WI	1,220	1,348	Private	$17,804
Belmont University	54%	TN	1,175	3,406	Private	$13,268
Biola University	54%	CA	1,130	3,465	Private	$11,442
Berry College	53%	GA	1,145	1,840	Private	$18,699
Bradley University	53%	IL	1,145	5,160	Private	$12,905
Bennington College	52%	VT	1,245	568	Private	$20,364
Baldwin-Wallace College	52%	OH	1,085	3,224	Private	$12,849
Bluffton University	50%	OH	1,010	1,030	Private	$11,773
Bryan College	50%	TN	1,105	744	Private	$10,563
Baylor University	49%	TX	1,200	11,585	Private	$14,738
Bellarmine University	49%	KY	1,085	1,940	Private	$11,463
Buena Vista University	47%	IA	1,025	2,377	Private	$9,546
Bethel College - Kansas	46%	KS	1,045	489	Private	$14,393
Baker University College of Arts and Sciences	43%	KS	1,085	879	Private	$27,534
Blue Mountain College	42%	MS	N/A	310	Private	$9,946
Bloomsburg University of Pennsylvania	42%	PA	1,015	7,432	Public	$7,766
Benedictine University	41%	IL	1,085	1,785	Private	$9,703
Briar Cliff University	41%	IA	1,010	1,012	Private	$10,571
Berklee College of Music	40%	MA	N/A	3,794	Private	$17,056
Berea College	40%	KY	1,065	1,551	Private	$20,798
Bethel College - Indiana	40%	IN	1,075	1,496	Private	$8,509
Benedictine College	40%	KS	1,105	1,269	Private	$6,694
Becker College	36%	MA	N/A	1,326	Private	$9,987
Bowling Green State University-Main Campus	34%	OH	1,010	15,369	Public	$9,108
Belmont Abbey College	34%	NC	1,025	828	Private	$9,579
Brigham Young University	32%	UT	1,220	28,573	Private	$14,443
Belhaven College	31%	MS	1,065	2,190	Private	$4,680
Ball State University	29%	IN	1,040	16,513	Public	$9,593
Blackburn College	29%	IL	1,010	594	Private	$8,528
Barton College	29%	NC	935	1,008	Private	$8,297
Bemidji State University	28%	MN	970	3,121	Public	$8,785
Brenau University	27%	GA	1,005	1,222	Private	$9,051
Bethany College - Kansas	26%	KS	1,025	564	Private	$10,546
Bluefield College	24%	VA	940	720	Private	$8,349
Burlington College	24%	VT	N/A	129	Private	$8,683

Name	4yr Grad Rate	State	Median SAT	Size	Sector	Student Related Exp./FTE
Bridgewater State College	23%	MA	1,020	6,907	Public	$7,095
Brigham Young University-Hawaii	23%	HI	1,065	2,328	Private	$16,095
Brescia University	21%	KY	970	484	Private	$10,320
Boricua College	20%	NY	N/A	1,091	Private	$4,548
Barry University	18%	FL	945	5,027	Private	$13,457
Bennett College for Women	17%	NC	805	568	Private	$20,871
Bluefield State College	16%	WV	930	1,503	Public	$3,480
Benedict College	16%	SC	N/A	2,511	Private	$9,803
Baker College of Flint	15%	MI	N/A	4,294	Private	$18,085
Bryn Athyn College of the New Church	15%	PA	1,100	136	Private	$25,326
Bowie State University	13%	MD	1,069	3,531	Public	$7,992
Bethune Cookman College	13%	FL	820	2,893	Private	$6,841
Bethel College - Tennessee	12%	TN	910	1,057	Private	$12,472
Brewton-Parker College	12%	GA	960	970	Private	$9,283
Black Hills State University	10%	SD	970	2,949	Public	$5,559
Bellevue University	8%	NE	N/A	3,382	Private	$4,970
Boise State University	6%	ID	1,005	12,801	Public	$6,992
Bloomfield College	6%	NJ	860	1,885	Private	$10,652
Baltimore Hebrew University Inc	N/A	MD	N/A	9	Private	$24,173
Bay Path College	N/A	MA	1,010	1,187	Private	$8,018
Boston Architectural Center	N/A	MA	N/A	542	Private	$9,270
Benjamin Franklin Institute of Technology	N/A	MA	N/A	363	Public	$9,648
Barnes-Jewish College of Nursing and Allied Health	N/A	MO	N/A	349	Private	$8,939
Barnard College	N/A	NY	1,370	2,316	Private	$22,076
Bryn Mawr College	N/A	PA	1,305	1,319	Private	$27,373
College of the Holy Cross	89%	MA	1,266	2,797	Private	$23,774
Carleton College	88%	MN	1,410	1,936	Private	$29,877
Columbia University in the City of New York	87%	NY	1,440	6,730	Private	$57,850
Colgate University	84%	NY	1,355	2,755	Private	$27,892
Cornell University	84%	NY	1,385	13,669	Private	$29,227
Colby College	84%	ME	1,355	1,871	Private	$28,812
College of William and Mary	83%	VA	1,350	5,549	Public	$12,201
Connecticut College	82%	CT	1,325	1,834	Private	$22,944
Claremont McKenna College	81%	CA	1,390	1,140	Private	$29,678
California Institute of Technology	81%	CA	1,510	913	Private	$89,266
Centre College	78%	KY	1,220	1,127	Private	$19,916
Cleveland Institute of Music	78%	OH	N/A	243	Private	$24,050

Name	4yr Grad Rate	State	Median SAT	Size	Sector	Student Related Exp./FTE
Colorado College	77%	CO	1,310	1,944	Private	$29,358
College of Saint Benedict	75%	MN	1,145	2,010	Private	$13,287
Carnegie Mellon University	69%	PA	1,380	5,464	Private	$33,957
Cardinal Stritch University	67%	WI	1,010	2,852	Private	$5,140
Champlain College	67%	VT	1,075	1,967	Private	$10,105
Coe College	64%	IA	1,165	1,274	Private	$14,045
Concordia College at Moorhead	64%	MN	1,105	2,718	Private	$12,223
Cooper Union for the Advancement of Science and Art	64%	NY	1,330	951	Private	$25,557
Clark University	63%	MA	1,205	2,150	Private	$16,769
Citadel Military College of South Carolina	62%	SC	1,075	2,153	Public	$10,940
College Misericordia	61%	PA	995	1,643	Private	$12,156
Central College	61%	IA	1,085	1,449	Private	$14,113
Creighton University	61%	NE	1,165	3,817	Private	$23,308
Cornell College	60%	IA	1,185	1,170	Private	$14,647
Catholic University of America	59%	DC	1,145	2,886	Private	$20,569
College of Saint Elizabeth	59%	NJ	925	849	Private	$13,540
Case Western Reserve University	59%	OH	1,340	3,792	Private	$30,672
Cedar Crest College	58%	PA	1,055	1,240	Private	$11,217
Cedarville University	58%	OH	1,145	2,983	Private	$13,953
California Lutheran University	57%	CA	1,085	1,954	Private	$11,017
College of Our Lady of the Elms	57%	MA	1,005	744	Private	$10,648
Clarke College	56%	IA	1,045	912	Private	$11,037
Calvin College	56%	MI	1,165	4,020	Private	$14,821
College of the Atlantic	55%	ME	1,206	302	Private	$18,994
Capital University	55%	OH	1,085	2,449	Private	$15,966
Colby-Sawyer College	54%	NH	1,010	960	Private	$17,220
Covenant College	52%	GA	1,165	1,156	Private	$10,549
College of the Ozarks	52%	MO	1,010	1,318	Private	$8,976
College of Notre Dame of Maryland	52%	MD	1,025	973	Private	$11,914
Canisius College	51%	NY	1,110	3,404	Private	$12,507
Clarkson University	51%	NY	1,150	2,638	Private	$16,257
Chestnut Hill College	49%	PA	965	881	Private	$12,583
Corcoran College of Art and Design	49%	DC	1,055	418	Private	$17,243
Concordia University - California	49%	CA	1,045	1,395	Private	$8,385
Chapman University	47%	CA	1,195	3,729	Private	$15,480
Corban College	47%	OR	1,103	703	Private	$10,701

Name	4yr Grad Rate	State	Median SAT	Size	Sector	Student Related Exp./FTE
California Baptist University	47%	CA	1,005	2,122	Private	$10,700
Carlow University	47%	PA	1,005	1,319	Private	$11,004
Carson-Newman College	47%	TN	1,045	1,794	Private	$10,463
Columbus College of Art and Design	46%	OH	970	1,322	Private	$9,305
Carthage College	46%	WI	1,105	2,295	Private	$10,745
Cabrini College	45%	PA	990	1,613	Private	$11,648
Concordia College - New York	45%	NY	950	611	Private	$9,491
California Institute of the Arts	45%	CA	N/A	822	Private	$24,940
Carroll College - Montana	45%	MT	1,085	1,314	Private	$9,413
Caldwell College	44%	NJ	960	1,272	Private	$10,507
College of Mount St. Joseph	44%	OH	970	1,537	Private	$11,602
Clemson University	44%	SC	1,205	13,537	Public	$10,532
Carroll College - Wisconsin	44%	WI	1,045	2,503	Private	$8,374
California Maritime Academy	43%	CA	1,080	754	Public	$18,161
Centenary College of Louisiana	43%	LA	1,145	889	Private	$19,168
College of Charleston	42%	SC	1,195	9,329	Public	$6,853
Claflin University	41%	SC	980	1,625	Private	$8,964
Cornish College of the Arts	40%	WA	N/A	749	Private	$14,336
Colorado School of Mines	40%	CO	1,220	3,052	Public	$12,088
College of St Catherine	40%	MN	1,045	2,776	Private	$11,819
Clearwater Christian College	40%	FL	1,045	559	Private	$7,548
Concordia University-Wisconsin	39%	WI	1,045	2,665	Private	$6,994
Chatham College	39%	PA	1,047	553	Private	$17,454
Centenary College	39%	NJ	930	1,695	Private	$8,428
Cazenovia College	38%	NY	995	884	Private	$13,266
Curry College	36%	MA	1,013	2,224	Private	$13,742
College of Mount Saint Vincent	35%	NY	1,015	1,342	Private	$11,592
Colorado State University	35%	CO	1,105	20,018	Public	$7,434
Culver-Stockton College	34%	MO	1,010	791	Private	$8,950
Concordia University - Oregon	34%	OR	1,010	874	Private	$7,016
Christian Brothers University	33%	TN	1,085	1,266	Private	$9,610
Central Methodist University-College of Liberal Arts & Sciences	32%	MO	970	799	Private	$11,672
Campbell University Inc	31%	NC	1,209	3,736	Private	$7,248
College of the Southwest	31%	NM	845	440	Private	$8,975
Columbia College - Missouri	30%	MO	1,010	7,633	Private	$4,170
Coker College	28%	SC	975	979	Private	$9,634
Cornerstone University	28%	MI	1,085	1,895	Private	$9,893
College of Santa Fe	28%	NM	1,070	874	Private	$14,568

Name	4yr Grad Rate	State	Median SAT	Size	Sector	Student Related Exp./FTE
College for Creative Studies	28%	MI	970	1,142	Private	$12,123
Campbellsville University	28%	KY	970	1,453	Private	$7,301
CUNY Bernard M Baruch College	27%	NY	1,110	10,783	Public	$7,737
Concordia University-Saint Paul	27%	MN	1,005	1,560	Private	$8,648
Catawba College	27%	NC	1,035	1,233	Private	$8,702
Clarion University of Pennsylvania	26%	PA	915	5,294	Public	$8,987
Central Missouri State University	26%	MO	1,010	7,718	Public	$9,633
Christopher Newport University	26%	VA	1,145	4,315	Public	$6,198
Columbia College Chicago	26%	IL	N/A	9,200	Private	$12,567
Cogswell Polytechnical College	26%	CA	N/A	184	Private	N/A
Central Washington University	26%	WA	1,028	8,895	Public	$7,709
Concordia University - Nebraska	26%	NE	1,085	1,118	Private	$7,598
California University of Pennsylvania	24%	PA	950	5,496	Public	$7,783
Charleston Southern University	24%	SC	975	2,333	Private	$8,727
CUNY Queens College	23%	NY	1,025	10,217	Public	$8,640
Castleton State College	23%	VT	990	1,753	Public	$7,911
College of St Joseph	23%	VT	1,005	208	Private	$10,201
California College of the Arts	23%	CA	1,105	1,265	Private	$16,590
Central Michigan University	21%	MI	1,010	18,412	Public	$6,628
Chadron State College	21%	NE	N/A	1,805	Public	$6,309
CUNY College of Staten Island	21%	NY	1,035	8,502	Public	$7,346
California State University-Stanislaus	20%	CA	970	5,159	Public	$8,443
Coastal Carolina University	20%	SC	1,040	5,968	Public	$7,320
California Polytechnic State University-San Luis Obispo	20%	CA	1,220	16,908	Public	$8,423
Clark Atlanta University	20%	GA	932	3,566	Private	$9,468
Chaminade University of Honolulu	19%	HI	950	1,666	Private	$8,264
Concordia University at Austin	19%	TX	1,015	878	Private	$9,412
Cascade College	18%	OR	990	278	Private	N/A
CUNY Brooklyn College	18%	NY	1,055	9,194	Public	$8,947
California State University-Chico	17%	CA	1,040	13,560	Public	$7,441
CUNY John Jay College Criminal Justice	17%	NY	940	10,355	Public	$5,951
Concordia University-Ann Arbor	17%	MI	1,045	524	Private	$13,452

Name	4yr Grad Rate	State	Median SAT	Size	Sector	Student Related Exp./FTE
Capitol College	16%	MD	950	259	Private	$9,612
California State University-East Bay	16%	CA	945	8,059	Public	$8,596
Colorado State University-Pueblo	16%	CO	N/A	3,895	Public	$5,539
Cumberland University	15%	TN	970	986	Private	$8,243
Cameron University	15%	OK	910	4,081	Public	$5,439
California State University-Fullerton	14%	CA	990	24,005	Public	$6,352
Columbia Union College	14%	MD	850	826	Private	$14,226
California State University-Bakersfield	14%	CA	940	5,266	Public	$8,119
CUNY Medgar Evers College	13%	NY	770	3,826	Public	$10,440
Concordia University - Illinois	13%	IL	1,025	985	Private	$11,158
Central State University	13%	OH	N/A	1,506	Public	$8,281
Concord University	13%	WV	970	2,352	Public	$5,242
California State University-San Bernardino	12%	CA	890	11,182	Public	$6,435
California State University-Fresno	12%	CA	960	15,757	Public	$7,816
California State University-Long Beach	12%	CA	1,015	24,663	Public	$7,536
Cheyney University of Pennsylvania	12%	PA	N/A	1,330	Public	$10,898
Columbus State University	12%	GA	1,000	5,149	Public	$6,569
College of Visual Arts	11%	MN	990	177	Private	$10,586
Cleveland State University	11%	OH	910	7,543	Public	$10,806
Central Connecticut State University	11%	CT	1,030	8,189	Public	$8,368
CUNY Hunter College	11%	NY	1,065	12,148	Public	$7,822
California State University-Los Angeles	11%	CA	895	12,255	Public	$7,446
California State Polytechnic University-Pomona	10%	CA	1,040	15,975	Public	$7,791
Clayton State University	10%	GA	985	4,305	Public	$6,972
California State University-Monterey Bay	10%	CA	1,000	3,184	Public	$10,515
California State University-Northridge	9%	CA	950	22,818	Public	$7,606
CUNY New York City College of Technology	9%	NY	N/A	8,884	Public	$7,801
California State University-Sacramento	9%	CA	965	19,715	Public	$7,325
CUNY Lehman College	8%	NY	927	6,227	Public	$10,245
Crichton College	8%	TN	970	646	Private	$7,263
California State University-San Marcos	8%	CA	985	5,227	Public	$8,135

Name	4yr Grad Rate	State	Median SAT	Size	Sector	Student Related Exp./FTE
California State University-Dominguez Hills	6%	CA	845	6,596	Public	$7,961
CUNY York College	6%	NY	838	4,535	Public	$8,625
Coppin State University	5%	MD	N/A	2,968	Public	$8,658
Clarkson College	4%	NE	990	460	Private	$15,715
CUNY City College	3%	NY	1,023	7,630	Public	$13,341
Chicago State University	3%	IL	890	4,024	Public	$12,486
Concordia College - Alabama	N/A	AL	N/A	750	Private	$3,939
Colorado Christian University	N/A	CO	1,065	1,325	Private	$11,920
Charter Oak State College	N/A	CT	N/A	634	Public	$6,361
Carlos Albizu University-Miami Campus	N/A	FL	N/A	254	Private	$7,621
Calumet College of Saint Joseph	N/A	IN	N/A	704	Private	$6,897
Cambridge College	N/A	MA	N/A	464	Private	$11,852
Cleary University	N/A	MI	950	447	Private	$7,171
College of Saint Mary	N/A	NE	970	689	Private	$11,030
Cabarrus College of Health Sciences	N/A	NC	1,025	242	Private	$12,370
Cincinnati College of Mortuary Science	N/A	OH	N/A	145	Private	$5,541
Cleveland Institute of Art	N/A	OH	1,025	521	Private	$12,467
Curtis Institute of Music	N/A	PA	N/A	147	Private	$34,200
Columbia College - South Carolina	N/A	SC	1,045	947	Private	$10,430
Converse College	N/A	SC	1,100	689	Private	$9,875
City University	N/A	WA	N/A	1,269	Private	$9,893
Duke University	90%	NC	1,430	6,491	Private	$50,476
Davidson College	89%	NC	1,360	1,683	Private	$27,784
Dartmouth College	86%	NH	1,450	4,070	Private	$53,547
DePauw University	79%	IN	1,230	2,366	Private	$24,175
Dickinson College	78%	PA	1,290	2,325	Private	$21,938
Denison University	75%	OH	1,240	2,301	Private	$25,083
Drew University	70%	NJ	1,200	1,578	Private	$20,657
DeSales University	59%	PA	1,080	1,802	Private	$11,046
Doane College	58%	NE	1,065	1,431	Private	$8,851
Duquesne University	58%	PA	1,125	5,432	Private	$12,105
Dominican University	57%	IL	1,045	1,210	Private	$13,089
Drake University	57%	IA	1,165	2,989	Private	$10,455
Dordt College	55%	IA	1,105	1,218	Private	$11,918
DePaul University	45%	IL	1,085	12,501	Private	$11,075
Drury University	43%	MO	1,165	3,420	Private	$8,405
Defiance College	43%	OH	990	724	Private	$10,606
Dominican University of	43%	CA	1,025	1,196	Private	$12,772

Name	4yr Grad Rate	State	Median SAT	Size	Sector	Student Related Exp./FTE
California						
Delaware Valley College	42%	PA	1,030	1,731	Private	$12,594
Dallas Baptist University	40%	TX	1,063	2,589	Private	$9,685
Dillard University	34%	LA	N/A	1,870	Private	$14,163
Dana College	33%	NE	1,010	659	Private	$10,292
Davis & Elkins College	31%	WV	950	581	Private	$13,055
Daniel Webster College	31%	NH	1,065	787	Private	$9,959
Dakota Wesleyan University	30%	SD	950	773	Private	$9,104
Dowling College	26%	NY	930	2,741	Private	$12,825
Dominican College of Blauvelt	26%	NY	890	1,205	Private	$11,146
Daemen College	24%	NY	1,010	1,382	Private	$10,708
Delta State University	24%	MS	930	2,951	Public	$7,508
Delaware State University	23%	DE	810	3,111	Public	$12,880
D'Youville College	19%	NY	975	1,262	Private	$9,606
Dakota State University	17%	SD	970	1,468	Public	$9,282
Drexel University	13%	PA	1,190	10,891	Private	$15,015
Davenport University	12%	MI	N/A	6,092	Private	$11,535
David N Myers University	12%	OH	N/A	688	Private	$7,554
Dickinson State University	11%	ND	930	2,009	Public	$5,555
Emory University	79%	GA	1,380	6,451	Private	$49,204
Emerson College	72%	MA	1,235	3,186	Private	$13,119
Elizabethtown College	65%	PA	1,115	1,963	Private	$15,350
Elon University	65%	NC	1,210	4,639	Private	$13,124
Erskine College and Seminary	65%	SC	1,110	588	Private	$8,414
Earlham College	62%	IN	1,225	1,209	Private	$17,369
Elmhurst College	61%	IL	1,085	2,472	Private	$13,288
Elmira College	57%	NY	1,140	1,280	Private	$13,837
Eastern University	57%	PA	1,080	2,091	Private	$9,840
Eckerd College	53%	FL	1,130	1,763	Private	$22,558
Emory and Henry College	50%	VA	1,060	1,010	Private	$12,468
Emmanuel College	50%	MA	1,070	1,742	Private	$11,635
Endicott College	49%	MA	1,070	1,786	Private	$9,879
Eastern Mennonite University	48%	VA	1,109	985	Private	$16,785
Eastern Nazarene College	42%	MA	1,040	1,080	Private	$9,915
Eureka College	41%	IL	1,025	515	Private	$11,873
Embry Riddle Aeronautical University-Daytona Beach	35%	FL	1,110	4,189	Private	$33,292
Eastern Illinois University	32%	IL	1,010	9,654	Public	$9,214
Elizabeth City State University	30%	NC	835	2,390	Public	$9,490
Embry Riddle Aeronautical University-Prescott	30%	AZ	1,148	1,528	Private	N/A
Edgewood College	30%	WI	1,025	1,686	Private	$11,612

Name	4yr Grad Rate	State	Median SAT	Size	Sector	Student Related Exp./FTE
East Carolina University	28%	NC	1,040	16,464	Public	$10,539
Emporia State University	25%	KS	990	3,982	Public	$7,815
Edinboro University of Pennsylvania	24%	PA	955	5,989	Public	$8,043
Eastern Connecticut State University	23%	CT	1,015	4,082	Public	$8,813
East Stroudsburg University of Pennsylvania	22%	PA	985	5,236	Public	$8,279
Eastern Washington University	21%	WA	1,220	8,650	Public	$7,526
Evangel University	19%	MO	1,085	1,693	Private	$8,302
Eastern Oregon University	17%	OR	995	2,290	Public	$7,619
East Tennessee State University	17%	TN	1,045	8,712	Public	$12,902
East Texas Baptist University	14%	TX	990	1,226	Private	$8,676
Eastern Michigan University	12%	MI	970	15,000	Public	$7,758
East Central University	12%	OK	970	3,374	Public	$4,852
Eastern Kentucky University	9%	KY	970	11,927	Public	$6,709
Eastern New Mexico University-Main Campus	8%	NM	905	2,770	Public	$7,457
East-West University	6%	IL	N/A	1,012	Private	$5,781
Edward Waters College	4%	FL	N/A	825	Private	$8,004
Furman University	80%	SC	1,270	2,734	Private	$21,447
Fairfield University	79%	CT	1,190	3,681	Private	$18,346
Franklin and Marshall College	75%	PA	1,275	1,996	Private	$24,672
Fordham University	73%	NY	1,190	7,101	Private	$18,159
Franciscan University of Steubenville	65%	OH	1,175	1,872	Private	$9,687
Franklin College	51%	IN	1,030	965	Private	$14,711
Fresno Pacific University	49%	CA	1,005	1,087	Private	$12,458
Florida State University	45%	FL	1,160	28,396	Public	$7,383
Franklin Pierce College	43%	NH	990	1,609	Private	$16,037
Flagler College	42%	FL	1,130	2,112	Private	$5,241
Florida Southern College	41%	FL	1,060	1,968	Private	$13,625
Florida Institute of Technology-Melbourne	40%	FL	1,170	2,295	Private	$12,981
Freed-Hardeman University	37%	TN	1,065	1,435	Private	$12,814
Fairleigh Dickinson University-College at Florham	36%	NJ	1,030	2,398	Private	N/A
Fontbonne University	35%	MO	1,010	1,724	Private	$8,793
Fort Hays State University	30%	KS	1,010	5,458	Public	$6,893
Fitchburg State College	27%	MA	1,000	3,184	Public	$7,760
Framingham State College	25%	MA	1,040	3,287	Public	$6,996
Fairleigh Dickinson University-Metropolitan Campus	25%	NJ	990	3,337	Private	$21,885
Friends University	23%	KS	990	1,917	Private	$7,301

Name	4yr Grad Rate	State	Median SAT	Size	Sector	Student Related Exp./FTE
Felician College	21%	NJ	910	1,288	Private	$10,494
Faulkner University	20%	AL	990	1,711	Private	$8,967
Florida International University	20%	FL	1,105	22,722	Public	$6,943
Frostburg State University	19%	MD	1,000	4,142	Public	$7,311
Florida Agricultural and Mechanical University	19%	FL	865	9,759	Public	$8,796
Ferrum College	17%	VA	925	972	Private	$11,463
Florida Memorial University	16%	FL	N/A	1,827	Private	$7,941
Francis Marion University	16%	SC	975	3,205	Public	$7,240
Farmingdale State University of New York	15%	NY	985	4,834	Public	$7,905
Fairmont State University	15%	WV	950	4,054	Public	$4,370
Florida Gulf Coast University	15%	FL	1,035	5,113	Public	$9,106
Fayetteville State University	14%	NC	840	4,422	Public	$8,360
Florida Atlantic University	14%	FL	1,040	15,058	Public	$8,884
Fort Valley State University	14%	GA	900	1,814	Public	$8,942
Ferris State University	14%	MI	970	9,724	Public	$9,110
Fort Lewis College	13%	CO	970	3,753	Public	$5,741
Florida Hospital College of Health Sciences	N/A	FL	N/A	1,062	Private	$7,158
Fashion Institute of Technology	N/A	NY	N/A	7,840	Public	$9,805
Franklin University	N/A	OH	N/A	3,406	Private	$5,085
Fisk University	N/A	TN	950	833	Private	$13,156
Georgetown University	90%	DC	1,390	6,576	Private	$27,283
Grinnell College	86%	IA	1,390	1,556	Private	$32,033
Grove City College	74%	PA	1,204	2,319	Private	N/A
Gettysburg College	74%	PA	1,275	2,486	Private	$22,942
George Washington University	72%	DC	1,280	10,081	Private	$21,593
Gonzaga University	65%	WA	1,190	4,042	Private	$13,705
Goucher College	62%	MD	1,205	1,319	Private	$16,499
Gustavus Adolphus College	60%	MN	1,165	2,516	Private	$16,250
George Fox University	59%	OR	1,115	1,656	Private	$13,063
Gordon College	57%	MA	1,200	1,566	Private	$14,683
Goldey-Beacom College	52%	DE	895	780	Private	$15,468
Guilford College	50%	NC	1,140	2,395	Private	$11,017
Gwynedd Mercy College	49%	PA	990	1,575	Private	$9,537
Grace College and Theological Seminary	48%	IN	1,055	1,029	Private	$7,266
Gannon University	48%	PA	1,045	2,314	Private	$12,571
Georgetown College	48%	KY	1,085	1,328	Private	$10,610
Goshen College	45%	IN	1,175	857	Private	$17,832
Geneva College	45%	PA	1,095	1,648	Private	$11,391

Name	4yr Grad Rate	State	Median SAT	Size	Sector	Student Related Exp./FTE
Greenville College	39%	IL	1,025	1,188	Private	$10,663
Georgian Court University	38%	NJ	940	1,563	Private	$11,815
Graceland University-Lamoni	36%	IA	990	1,595	Private	$12,322
Georgia Institute of Technology-Main Campus	34%	GA	1,335	11,275	Public	$13,102
Greensboro College	32%	NC	980	967	Private	$13,812
George Mason University	31%	VA	1,105	15,082	Public	$9,655
Gardner-Webb University	31%	NC	1,015	2,285	Private	$8,996
Grand View College	28%	IA	950	1,494	Private	$9,305
Georgia College and State University	23%	GA	1,115	4,431	Public	$7,927
Grace Bible College	23%	MI	950	154	Private	$11,487
Green Mountain College	21%	VT	950	675	Private	$13,232
Grambling State University	20%	LA	N/A	4,296	Public	$7,315
Grand Valley State University	19%	MI	1,085	17,272	Public	$7,376
Georgia State University	15%	GA	1,090	15,501	Public	$8,918
Georgia Southwestern State University	14%	GA	995	1,879	Public	$8,078
Georgia Southern University	13%	GA	1,065	13,629	Public	$6,039
Glenville State College	10%	WV	910	1,216	Public	$5,000
Gallaudet University	7%	DC	775	1,195	Private	$44,942
Golden Gate University-San Francisco	N/A	CA	N/A	279	Private	$17,643
Granite State College	N/A	NH	N/A	788	Public	$12,949
Goddard College	N/A	VT	N/A	165	Private	$6,126
Haverford College	91%	PA	1,380	1,168	Private	$31,584
Harvard University	87%	MA	1,490	7,973	Private	$51,857
Hamilton College	83%	NY	1,355	1,801	Private	$30,834
Harvey Mudd College	78%	CA	1,470	742	Private	$32,192
Hood College	69%	MD	1,105	1,066	Private	$14,072
Hobart William Smith Colleges	68%	NY	1,170	1,866	Private	$22,624
Hope College	64%	MI	1,185	3,066	Private	$13,821
Hampden-Sydney College	62%	VA	1,160	1,060	Private	$19,127
Hanover College	62%	IN	1,195	1,005	Private	$18,232
Houghton College	61%	NY	1,170	1,357	Private	$14,625
Hendrix College	60%	AR	1,240	1,008	Private	$17,436
Hamline University	53%	MN	1,105	1,979	Private	$14,431
Hiram College	53%	OH	1,065	945	Private	$13,695
Huntington University	49%	IN	1,075	869	Private	$15,475
Hastings College	48%	NE	1,065	1,129	Private	$10,760
Hampshire College	47%	MA	1,265	1,376	Private	$15,066
Howard University	46%	DC	1,125	6,899	Private	$23,071
High Point University	45%	NC	1,025	2,391	Private	$8,224

Name	4yr Grad Rate	State	Median SAT	Size	Sector	Student Related Exp./FTE
Huntingdon College - Alabama	44%	AL	1,045	752	Private	$12,695
Hilbert College	44%	NY	920	923	Private	$7,950
Hartwick College	44%	NY	1,135	1,424	Private	$17,694
Heidelberg College	44%	OH	1,010	1,196	Private	$11,408
Holy Names University	40%	CA	990	539	Private	$12,513
Hampton University	40%	VA	1,084	5,050	Private	$10,888
Harding University	37%	AR	1,065	3,967	Private	$9,438
Hofstra University	36%	NY	1,140	8,315	Private	$14,886
Hannibal-Lagrange College	35%	MO	1,045	873	Private	$6,393
Houston Baptist University	33%	TX	1,115	1,746	Private	$9,983
Hope International University	29%	CA	990	722	Private	$11,099
Hardin-Simmons University	28%	TX	1,040	1,872	Private	$8,716
Hawaii Pacific University	27%	HI	1,000	4,914	Private	$8,958
Howard Payne University	24%	TX	1,027	1,150	Private	$10,163
Humphreys College-Stockton	20%	CA	N/A	663	Private	$5,010
Husson College	18%	ME	928	1,523	Private	$7,407
Henderson State University	18%	AR	1,025	2,838	Public	$5,883
Humboldt State University	12%	CA	1,065	6,087	Public	$9,109
Harris-Stowe State University	2%	MO	N/A	1,201	Public	$9,178
Hellenic College-Holy Cross Greek Orthodox School of Theology	N/A	MA	N/A	83	Private	$17,773
Holy Family University	N/A	PA	950	1,664	Private	$9,406
Huston-Tillotson University	N/A	TX	755	642	Private	$10,187
Hollins University	N/A	VA	1,125	809	Private	$21,037
Henry Cogswell College	N/A	WA	1,120	145	Private	$24,016
Heritage University	N/A	WA	N/A	647	Private	$10,227
Illinois Wesleyan University	76%	IL	1,280	2,142	Private	$20,848
Ithaca College	69%	NY	1,180	6,007	Private	$14,552
Indiana Wesleyan University	63%	IN	1,087	8,050	Private	$4,962
Indiana University-Bloomington	50%	IN	1,110	28,503	Public	$11,348
Iona College	47%	NY	1,125	3,203	Private	$11,066
Illinois College	43%	IL	1,105	1,017	Private	$12,591
Illinois Institute of Technology	40%	IL	1,280	2,064	Private	$18,315
Illinois State University	37%	IL	1,105	17,043	Public	$8,199
Iowa State University	31%	IA	1,105	19,866	Public	$9,492
Indiana University of Pennsylvania-Main Campus	23%	PA	1,040	11,498	Public	$8,753
Indiana State University	20%	IN	945	7,975	Public	$8,830
Indiana Institute of Technology	16%	IN	940	1,932	Private	$5,582
Iowa Wesleyan College	9%	IA	885	692	Private	$6,776

Name	4yr Grad Rate	State	Median SAT	Size	Sector	Student Related Exp./FTE
International College (FL)	9%	FL	N/A	1,193	Private	$10,423
Indiana University-Kokomo	9%	IN	975	1,861	Public	$6,227
Indiana University-Northwest	8%	IN	905	3,108	Public	$6,900
Indiana University-Southeast	8%	IN	965	3,913	Public	$6,123
Indiana University-Purdue University-Indianapolis	8%	IN	995	16,303	Public	$16,571
Indiana University-East	6%	IN	915	1,659	Public	$6,179
Idaho State University	5%	ID	N/A	9,047	Public	$8,664
Indiana University-Purdue University-Fort Wayne	4%	IN	980	8,218	Public	$5,741
Indiana University-South Bend	4%	IN	960	4,532	Public	$6,804
Immaculata University	N/A	PA	970	1,466	Private	$10,833
Jewish Theological Seminary of America	94%	NY	1,331	199	Private	$27,597
Johns Hopkins University	82%	MD	1,385	5,309	Private	$88,013
Juniata College	74%	PA	1,175	1,409	Private	$14,689
John Carroll University	65%	OH	1,085	3,224	Private	$13,003
James Madison University	65%	VA	1,160	15,129	Public	$7,102
Johnson & Wales University-Denver	54%	CO	N/A	1,529	Private	N/A
John Brown University	51%	AR	1,145	1,607	Private	$10,182
Johnson & Wales University	41%	RI	N/A	8,712	Private	$15,131
Judson College (IL)	39%	IL	N/A	1,008	Private	$11,166
Jacksonville University	38%	FL	1,000	2,145	Private	$13,710
Jamestown College	32%	ND	1,025	982	Private	$7,466
Johnson & Wales University-Florida Campus	32%	FL	N/A	2,362	Private	N/A
Johnson C Smith University	31%	NC	912	1,361	Private	$14,378
Johnson State College	17%	VT	965	1,203	Public	$8,966
Jacksonville State University	15%	AL	930	6,304	Public	$6,984
Jackson State University	14%	MS	865	6,033	Public	$7,237
Judson College (AL)	N/A	AL	1,005	282	Private	$15,528
Jarvis Christian College	N/A	TX	N/A	563	Private	$9,169
Johnson & Wales University-Charlotte	N/A	NC	N/A	2,152	Private	N/A
Kenyon College	85%	OH	1,330	1,647	Private	$23,111
Kalamazoo College	76%	MI	1,280	1,263	Private	$19,686
Kansas City Art Institute	71%	MO	1,085	586	Private	$10,044
Knox College	70%	IL	1,240	1,227	Private	$17,024
King's College	62%	PA	1,035	1,936	Private	$12,988
King College	51%	TN	1,030	826	Private	$11,684
Keuka College	30%	NY	965	1,166	Private	$9,836
Kutztown University of Pennsylvania	28%	PA	995	8,236	Public	$7,346

Name	4yr Grad Rate	State	Median SAT	Size	Sector	Student Related Exp./FTE
Kendall College	27%	IL	1,010	591	Private	$18,398
Keene State College	26%	NH	1,000	4,356	Public	$8,518
Kansas Wesleyan University	26%	KS	1,065	721	Private	$8,009
Kansas State University	24%	KS	1,065	17,292	Public	$8,836
Kentucky Wesleyan College	23%	KY	1,005	730	Private	$9,800
Kent State University-Kent Campus	21%	OH	1,010	16,800	Public	$8,355
Kentucky Christian University	19%	KY	1,010	563	Private	$5,556
Keystone College	17%	PA	900	1,355	Private	$8,462
Kentucky State University	16%	KY	825	1,822	Public	$11,551
Kean University	16%	NJ	950	8,406	Public	$9,197
Kettering University	11%	MI	1,185	2,411	Private	$12,100
Kennesaw State University	7%	GA	1,055	13,184	Public	$6,184
Lafayette College	88%	PA	1,275	2,303	Private	$30,216
Loyola College in Maryland	77%	MD	1,220	3,519	Private	$16,145
Lehigh University	75%	PA	1,320	4,640	Private	$23,498
Lester L Cox College of Nursing and Health Science	71%	MO	N/A	383	Private	$8,355
Linfield College	65%	OR	1,145	1,722	Private	$19,463
Luther College	63%	IA	1,145	2,499	Private	$13,103
Lebanon Valley College	62%	PA	1,120	1,667	Private	$12,898
Lawrence University	62%	WI	1,240	1,405	Private	$20,800
Loyola University Chicago	61%	IL	1,125	8,625	Private	$15,389
Loyola Marymount University	59%	CA	1,170	5,495	Private	$16,908
Lycoming College	59%	PA	1,060	1,467	Private	$12,373
Lewis & Clark College	59%	OR	1,280	1,949	Private	$19,682
La Salle University	59%	PA	1,073	3,670	Private	$12,441
Le Moyne College	58%	NY	1,100	2,475	Private	$11,833
Lyon College	58%	AR	1,165	468	Private	$20,807
Lake Forest College	58%	IL	N/A	1,405	Private	$17,213
La Roche College	57%	PA	945	1,301	Private	$9,486
Loras College	56%	IA	1,045	1,539	Private	$11,536
Loyola University New Orleans	52%	LA	N/A	N/A	Private	$14,208
LaGrange College	48%	GA	1,020	927	Private	$16,538
Lasell College	46%	MA	975	1,201	Private	$9,263
Longwood University	46%	VA	1,070	3,650	Public	$6,206
Lenoir-Rhyne College	46%	NC	1,030	1,345	Private	$11,991
Lynchburg College	43%	VA	1,055	1,966	Private	$12,156
Laguna College of Art and Design	40%	CA	N/A	312	Private	$9,829
Liberty University	36%	VA	1,010	8,943	Private	$7,191
LeTourneau University	34%	TX	1,160	2,140	Private	$13,903
Lesley University	34%	MA	1,045	1,324	Private	$19,818

Name	4yr Grad Rate	State	Median SAT	Size	Sector	Student Related Exp./FTE
Lewis University	32%	IL	1,025	2,972	Private	$10,420
Lambuth University	31%	TN	1,085	779	Private	$10,286
Lake Erie College	30%	OH	930	610	Private	$10,602
Lincoln Memorial University	30%	TN	970	1,113	Private	$6,410
Lipscomb University	30%	TN	1,105	2,147	Private	$14,685
Lock Haven University of Pennsylvania	29%	PA	950	4,696	Public	$8,182
Lindenwood University	29%	MO	1,045	5,307	Private	$4,217
Lee University	29%	TN	1,070	3,426	Private	$6,848
Louisiana Tech University	28%	LA	1,045	8,171	Public	$4,931
Lynn University	26%	FL	915	2,188	Private	$14,662
Long Island University-C W Post Campus	25%	NY	990	5,199	Private	$16,272
Lawrence Technological University	24%	MI	1,025	1,957	Private	$14,118
Louisiana State University and Agricultural & Mechanical College	24%	LA	1,125	26,529	Public	$8,604
Limestone College	24%	SC	975	2,432	Private	$5,244
Louisiana College	23%	LA	1,030	899	Private	$10,909
Lakeland College	23%	WI	970	2,058	Private	$7,666
Lyndon State College	23%	VT	939	1,199	Public	$8,046
Lubbock Christian University	20%	TX	990	1,534	Private	$6,766
Lake Superior State University	19%	MI	990	2,483	Public	$6,450
La Sierra University	19%	CA	970	1,515	Private	$11,314
Langston University	19%	OK	N/A	2,599	Public	$6,550
Lamar University	18%	TX	N/A	7,753	Public	$5,840
Lincoln University of Pennsylvania	18%	PA	820	1,673	Public	$12,611
Lane College	17%	TN	825	1,206	Private	$4,649
Lander University	17%	SC	970	2,381	Public	$6,820
Lees-McRae College	17%	NC	950	872	Private	$10,686
Louisiana State University-Shreveport	13%	LA	950	3,095	Public	$5,736
Lourdes College	13%	OH	910	1,137	Private	$6,789
Livingstone College	12%	NC	730	874	Private	$7,825
Lindsey Wilson College	12%	KY	N/A	1,512	Private	$6,840
Lincoln University - Missouri	10%	MO	N/A	2,329	Public	$6,672
Lewis-Clark State College	7%	ID	930	2,671	Public	$8,174
Long Island University-Brooklyn Campus	5%	NY	945	4,699	Private	$17,096
Le Moyne-Owen College	3%	TN	N/A	726	Private	$12,219
Middlebury College	88%	VT	1,330	2,432	Private	$36,857
Muhlenberg College	83%	PA	1,230	2,330	Private	$18,451

Name	4yr Grad Rate	State	Median SAT	Size	Sector	Student Related Exp./FTE
Massachusetts Institute of Technology	82%	MA	1,500	4,031	Private	$60,139
MacAlester College	81%	MN	1,355	1,841	Private	$24,430
Mount Holyoke College	79%	MA	1,317	2,078	Private	$30,635
Marist College	70%	NY	1,175	4,574	Private	$12,581
Miami University-Oxford	68%	OH	1,220	14,725	Public	$12,910
Messiah College	68%	PA	1,200	2,881	Private	$15,779
Mount St Mary's University	67%	MD	1,100	1,542	Private	$12,928
McDaniel College	66%	MD	1,050	1,662	Private	$12,926
Moravian College and Moravian Theological Seminary	65%	PA	1,145	1,626	Private	$15,877
Monmouth College	61%	IL	1,085	1,334	Private	$11,769
Millsaps College	60%	MS	1,205	1,054	Private	$16,035
Mills College	59%	CA	1,135	855	Private	$23,393
Manhattan College	58%	NY	1,125	2,928	Private	$13,778
Maryland Institute College of Art	58%	MD	1,160	1,610	Private	$13,638
Marquette University	58%	WI	1,205	7,690	Private	$14,927
Millikin University	57%	IL	1,065	2,497	Private	$9,770
Mount St Mary's College	56%	CA	920	1,640	Private	$13,244
Merrimack College	55%	MA	1,075	1,982	Private	$14,521
Meredith College	54%	NC	1,035	1,768	Private	$15,596
Mount Mercy College	53%	IA	1,030	1,178	Private	$12,129
Manhattanville College	53%	NY	1,100	1,701	Private	$13,133
Maryville University of Saint Louis	53%	MO	1,105	1,960	Private	$11,133
Mercyhurst College	52%	PA	1,075	3,532	Private	$9,168
Milligan College	52%	TN	1,085	738	Private	$10,041
Mary Baldwin College	51%	VA	1,055	1,180	Private	$11,707
Midland Lutheran College	51%	NE	1,010	907	Private	$9,391
Manhattan School of Music	51%	NY	N/A	411	Private	$21,691
Marietta College	51%	OH	1,065	1,303	Private	$16,064
Maryville College	50%	TN	1,125	1,129	Private	$11,538
Mount Union College	50%	OH	1,045	2,082	Private	$10,687
Mississippi College	46%	MS	1,065	2,337	Private	$9,842
Muskingum College	45%	OH	1,010	1,587	Private	$10,259
Michigan State University	44%	MI	1,125	33,359	Public	$11,777
MidAmerica Nazarene University	44%	KS	1,045	1,251	Private	$6,612
Milwaukee Institute of Art Design	43%	WI	N/A	619	Private	$11,401
Manchester College	43%	IN	1,020	1,069	Private	$13,109
Massachusetts College of Art	42%	MA	1,105	1,583	Public	$11,454

Name	4yr Grad Rate	State	Median SAT	Size	Sector	Student Related Exp./FTE
Massachusetts Maritime Academy	41%	MA	1,050	938	Public	$14,391
Massachusetts College of Pharmacy & Health Science	41%	MA	1,045	535	Private	$15,144
Malone College	41%	OH	1,025	1,757	Private	$8,039
Maine College of Art	40%	ME	1,045	444	Private	$15,825
Marywood University	39%	PA	1,035	1,730	Private	$12,724
Marymount University	39%	VA	1,002	2,021	Private	$11,709
Murray State University	39%	KY	1,025	7,629	Public	$7,647
Mount Vernon Nazarene University	38%	OH	1,045	2,012	Private	$10,265
Mount Saint Mary College	38%	NY	1,005	1,756	Private	$8,719
Marlboro College	37%	VT	1,170	332	Private	$18,823
Millersville University of Pennsylvania	37%	PA	1,060	6,513	Public	$8,016
McKendree College	37%	IL	1,025	1,830	Private	$9,420
Monmouth University	37%	NJ	1,075	4,263	Private	$11,857
Massachusetts College of Liberal Arts	36%	MA	1,038	1,281	Public	$11,888
Metropolitan College of New York	36%	NY	N/A	1,145	Private	$10,689
Marian College of Fond du Lac	35%	WI	950	1,600	Private	$9,207
Montserrat College of Art	34%	MA	1,012	289	Private	$12,029
Milwaukee School of Engineering	34%	WI	1,165	1,910	Private	$13,822
Morningside College	34%	IA	1,025	1,094	Private	$11,261
Madonna University	34%	MI	1,125	2,239	Private	$9,125
Morehouse College	33%	GA	1,090	2,914	Private	$12,534
Molloy College	33%	NY	1,023	2,157	Private	$12,294
Mitchell College	31%	CT	N/A	672	Private	$11,812
Mercer University	30%	GA	1,180	4,030	Private	$15,800
Marymount Manhattan College	30%	NY	1,070	1,738	Private	$11,589
Mount Marty College - South Dakota	30%	SD	1,025	838	Private	$7,423
Mansfield University of Pennsylvania	30%	PA	975	2,805	Public	$8,565
Mississippi University for Women	30%	MS	990	1,824	Public	$9,649
Mount Aloysius College	29%	PA	930	1,259	Private	$9,197
Marian College	29%	IN	1,020	1,281	Private	$10,159
MacMurray College	28%	IL	950	661	Private	$12,482
Mississippi State University	27%	MS	1,065	11,584	Public	$7,163
McMurry University	27%	TX	985	1,265	Private	$8,797
Mount Mary College - Wisconsin	27%	WI	905	1,098	Private	$10,407

Name	4yr Grad Rate	State	Median SAT	Size	Sector	Student Related Exp./FTE
Memphis College of Art	27%	TN	970	285	Private	$9,916
Montclair State University	27%	NJ	1,045	10,664	Public	$7,652
Mount Olive College	26%	NC	N/A	2,241	Private	$5,569
Michigan Technological University	26%	MI	1,165	5,310	Public	$9,843
Mars Hill College	25%	NC	995	1,237	Private	$6,005
Maharishi University of Management	25%	IA	N/A	210	Private	$6,846
Middle Tennessee State University	25%	TN	1,030	18,324	Public	$7,469
Missouri State University	25%	MO	1,085	13,806	Public	$6,400
Missouri Baptist University	23%	MO	950	1,963	Private	$4,781
Medaille College	21%	NY	967	1,646	Private	$7,618
Miles College	21%	AL	N/A	1,668	Private	$7,150
Montana State University-Bozeman	19%	MT	1,065	9,784	Public	$7,074
Minnesota State University-Mankato	19%	MN	1,010	11,785	Public	$7,145
Morgan State University	18%	MD	895	5,316	Public	$8,141
Morris College	18%	SC	N/A	850	Private	$7,963
Missouri Southern State University	18%	MO	1,010	4,387	Public	$6,561
Montana State University-Northern	18%	MT	905	1,091	Public	$9,858
Marshall University	17%	WV	1,045	8,740	Public	$7,864
Montreat College	17%	NC	980	948	Private	$7,789
Missouri Valley College	17%	MO	925	1,453	Private	$4,614
Metropolitan State University	16%	MN	N/A	3,327	Public	$8,240
Minnesota State University-Moorhead	16%	MN	1,010	6,546	Public	$6,500
Morehead State University	16%	KY	910	6,473	Public	$7,454
McPherson College	16%	KS	1,010	445	Private	$14,163
Mercy College-Main Campus	16%	NY	N/A	4,341	Private	$9,581
Mayville State University	15%	ND	910	723	Public	$6,034
Menlo College	15%	CA	940	704	Private	$12,984
Methodist College	15%	NC	990	1,802	Private	$8,309
Mount Ida College	14%	MA	880	1,236	Private	$12,660
Mississippi Valley State University	14%	MS	805	2,539	Public	$6,497
Minot State University	14%	ND	970	2,831	Public	$6,359
Mesa State College	11%	CO	970	5,025	Public	$3,980
McNeese State University	11%	LA	930	6,953	Public	$4,866
Midway College	10%	KY	N/A	1,010	Private	$7,948
Missouri Western State University	10%	MO	910	4,283	Public	$7,132

Name	4yr Grad Rate	State	Median SAT	Size	Sector	Student Related Exp./FTE
Mountain State University	10%	WV	910	3,295	Private	$5,137
Midwestern State University	9%	TX	975	4,523	Public	$5,904
Montana State University-Billings	9%	MT	990	2,808	Public	$8,804
Marylhurst University	8%	OR	N/A	452	Private	$11,349
Montana Tech of the University of Montana	8%	MT	1,030	1,497	Public	$8,594
Metropolitan State College of Denver	6%	CO	930	15,408	Public	$4,387
Martin University	N/A	IN	N/A	311	Private	$9,960
Mercy College of Health Sciences	N/A	IA	970	495	Private	$8,831
Maine Maritime Academy	N/A	ME	1,025	811	Public	$9,903
Marygrove College	N/A	MI	865	509	Private	$3,442
Minneapolis College of Art and Design	N/A	MN	1,045	635	Private	$17,470
Moore College of Art and Design	N/A	PA	985	436	Private	$13,222
Northwestern University	86%	IL	1,410	8,391	Private	$38,085
New York University	78%	NY	1,330	19,509	Private	$31,775
New College of California	72%	CA	N/A	300	Private	$12,874
Nazareth College of Rochester	61%	NY	1,150	1,928	Private	$12,559
Niagara University	56%	NY	1,050	2,858	Private	$8,441
Nebraska Wesleyan University	56%	NE	1,085	1,685	Private	$11,369
Northwestern College - Iowa	53%	IA	1,105	1,242	Private	$11,967
North Central College	51%	IL	1,125	1,984	Private	$12,259
North Carolina School of the Arts	50%	NC	1,108	722	Public	$20,844
Northwestern College - Minnesota	42%	MN	1,085	2,325	Private	$8,547
North Park University	41%	IL	1,045	1,683	Private	$12,612
Notre Dame de Namur University	39%	CA	980	717	Private	$13,431
Northland College	39%	WI	1,125	676	Private	$13,072
Norwich University	38%	VT	1,075	1,880	Private	$13,267
Northwest University	37%	WA	1,045	1,085	Private	$8,557
North Carolina State University at Raleigh	37%	NC	1,195	20,406	Public	$11,851
Northwood University - Michigan	36%	MI	950	2,917	Private	$15,282
New England College	36%	NH	885	995	Private	$11,366
Nichols College	35%	MA	880	1,019	Private	$10,524
Nova Southeastern University	34%	FL	1,040	4,070	Private	$17,038
North Georgia College & State University	32%	GA	1,075	3,634	Public	$7,039
Newberry College	32%	SC	970	828	Private	$11,486

Name	4yr Grad Rate	State	Median SAT	Size	Sector	Student Related Exp./FTE
Northwest Missouri State University	31%	MO	1,010	4,931	Public	$8,076
Northwest Nazarene University	31%	ID	N/A	1,103	Private	$11,698
Neumann College	29%	PA	880	1,992	Private	$9,275
Newman University	29%	KS	1,045	1,326	Private	$6,629
Nyack College	28%	NY	925	1,812	Private	$11,785
Northern Arizona University	27%	AZ	1,000	11,804	Public	$8,736
Northwest Christian College	27%	OR	976	305	Private	$18,435
Northwood University - Texas	23%	TX	930	897	Private	N/A
Northern Illinois University	23%	IL	1,030	17,228	Public	$6,820
North Carolina Central University	23%	NC	840	5,454	Public	$9,656
New Mexico Institute of Mining and Technology	22%	NM	1,205	1,213	Public	$11,231
North Carolina Wesleyan College	21%	NC	995	1,457	Private	$8,023
Naropa University	21%	CO	1,105	429	Private	$11,983
North Carolina A & T State University	19%	NC	890	9,149	Public	$7,970
New York Institute of Technology-Old Westbury	19%	NY	1,105	3,213	Private	$14,618
New Jersey Institute of Technology	19%	NJ	1,125	4,476	Public	$10,750
Northwood University-Florida Education Center	18%	FL	930	837	Private	N/A
North Dakota State University-Main Campus	18%	ND	1,065	9,432	Public	$6,376
Northern Michigan University	17%	MI	1,025	8,097	Public	$6,682
Northern State University	16%	SD	950	1,872	Public	$9,305
Notre Dame College	16%	OH	910	754	Private	$8,651
Newbury College-Brookline	14%	MA	N/A	1,035	Private	$7,099
Northwestern Oklahoma State University	14%	OK	970	1,605	Public	$5,993
Northwestern State University of Louisiana	14%	LA	930	7,236	Public	$5,071
New Mexico State University-Main Campus	12%	NM	970	11,044	Public	$7,045
Norfolk State University	12%	VA	880	4,726	Public	$9,014
Northeastern State University	12%	OK	970	7,078	Public	$4,883
National University	10%	CA	N/A	3,261	Private	$5,604
Northern Kentucky University	10%	KY	970	10,131	Public	$6,821
New York Institute of Technology-Manhattan Campus	10%	NY	1,055	1,576	Private	N/A
New Mexico Highlands University	10%	NM	870	1,493	Public	$9,457

Name	4yr Grad Rate	State	Median SAT	Size	Sector	Student Related Exp./FTE
Nicholls State University	9%	LA	950	5,963	Public	$5,196
New Jersey City University	7%	NJ	905	4,796	Public	$11,437
North Central University	5%	MN	990	1,166	Private	$6,526
Northeastern Illinois University	3%	IL	885	6,611	Public	$6,469
National-Louis University	1%	IL	870	1,779	Private	$11,152
Northeastern University	N/A	MA	1,230	15,751	Private	$14,911
Nebraska Methodist College of Nursing & Allied Health	N/A	NE	990	417	Private	$16,163
New College of Florida	N/A	FL	1,300	761	Public	$13,567
Occidental College	75%	CA	1,295	1,802	Private	$20,243
Oberlin College	70%	OH	1,365	2,785	Private	$30,557
Ohio Wesleyan University	60%	OH	1,220	1,951	Private	$19,202
Oklahoma Baptist University	57%	OK	885	1,486	Private	$10,597
Oglethorpe University	53%	GA	1,105	930	Private	$14,353
Ohio Northern University	51%	OH	1,165	2,549	Private	$15,358
Ohio University-Main Campus	47%	OH	1,065	16,465	Public	$10,351
Ouachita Baptist University	43%	AR	1,085	1,434	Private	$11,646
Oral Roberts University	42%	OK	1,065	2,712	Private	$6,968
Otterbein College	41%	OH	1,085	2,413	Private	$12,546
Olivet Nazarene University	40%	IL	1,045	2,681	Private	$9,682
Oklahoma City University	39%	OK	1,125	1,716	Private	$12,994
Ohio State University-Main Campus	39%	OH	1,185	35,015	Public	$15,391
Otis College of Art and Design	34%	CA	1,035	1,027	Private	$15,500
Ohio Valley University	31%	WV	970	517	Private	$11,105
Oakland City University	30%	IN	985	1,372	Private	$4,655
Oklahoma Panhandle State University	29%	OK	990	995	Public	$5,562
Oregon State University	29%	OR	1,080	14,374	Public	$9,034
Oklahoma State University-Main Campus	27%	OK	1,125	17,532	Public	$7,792
Ottawa University	27%	KS	1,010	422	Private	$31,345
Ohio Dominican University	27%	OH	1,010	1,988	Private	$7,566
Oklahoma Wesleyan University	24%	OK	N/A	725	Private	$10,794
Oakwood College	24%	AL	885	1,623	Private	$10,882
Old Dominion University	23%	VA	1,060	12,310	Public	$8,646
Oklahoma Christian University	22%	OK	1,070	1,648	Private	$9,845
Olivet College	20%	MI	885	1,038	Private	$8,712
Oregon Institute of Technology	17%	OR	1,055	2,363	Public	$8,337
Our Lady of the Lake University-San Antonio	16%	TX	945	1,425	Private	$15,497

Name	4yr Grad Rate	State	Median SAT	Size	Sector	Student Related Exp./FTE
Ohio State University-Lima Campus	15%	OH	N/A	927	Public	$8,416
Ohio State University-Marion Campus	13%	OH	N/A	1,241	Public	$6,277
Oakland University	13%	MI	1,010	10,989	Public	$6,977
Ohio State University-Newark Campus	13%	OH	950	1,873	Public	$5,284
Ohio State University-Mansfield Campus	11%	OH	N/A	1,204	Public	$6,251
Our Lady of Holy Cross College	4%	LA	N/A	N/A	Private	N/A
Oglala Lakota College	N/A	SD	N/A	826	Public	$8,183
Princeton University	89%	NJ	1,480	4,761	Private	$46,891
Pomona College	87%	CA	1,455	1,533	Private	$37,748
Providence College	83%	RI	1,195	4,123	Private	$12,548
Pepperdine University	71%	CA	1,225	2,893	Private	$22,887
Pitzer College	68%	CA	1,225	930	Private	$30,055
Presbyterian College	65%	SC	1,135	1,157	Private	$16,443
Principia College	65%	IL	1,180	538	Private	$33,061
Pennsylvania State University-Main Campus	56%	PA	1,190	33,684	Public	$13,984
Pacific University	52%	OR	1,125	1,193	Private	$14,780
Point Loma Nazarene University	51%	CA	1,155	2,309	Private	$13,209
Pacific Lutheran University	51%	WA	1,120	3,237	Private	$12,704
Point Park University	44%	PA	1,025	2,464	Private	$11,081
Pittsburg State University	44%	KS	1,010	5,270	Public	$6,773
Piedmont College	42%	GA	1,035	876	Private	$7,893
Presentation College	42%	SD	950	594	Private	$7,620
Philadelphia University	41%	PA	1,070	2,524	Private	$13,678
Pratt Institute-Main	40%	NY	1,100	3,120	Private	$13,265
Pace University-New York	39%	NY	1,075	7,562	Private	$17,790
Pennsylvania State University-Penn State Erie-Behrend College	37%	PA	1,055	3,234	Public	N/A
Purdue University-Main Campus	37%	IN	1,145	30,579	Public	$11,898
Pennsylvania State University-Penn State Altoona	36%	PA	1,015	3,441	Public	N/A
Pine Manor College	35%	MA	835	450	Private	$13,885
Palm Beach Atlantic University-West Palm Beach	35%	FL	1,010	2,352	Private	$9,215
Pacific Northwest College of Art	33%	OR	N/A	268	Private	$16,251
Pfeiffer University	31%	NC	990	1,104	Private	$8,766
Polytechnic University	29%	NY	1,175	1,474	Private	$22,402

Name	4yr Grad Rate	State	Median SAT	Size	Sector	Student Related Exp./FTE
Plymouth State University	27%	NH	960	4,035	Public	$8,186
Pennsylvania College of Technology	25%	PA	920	5,856	Public	$11,307
Pacific Union College	24%	CA	1,110	1,430	Private	$12,652
Prescott College	22%	AZ	1,150	743	Private	$10,107
Pikeville College	17%	KY	N/A	800	Private	$10,470
Philadelphia Biblical University-Langhorne	15%	PA	1,060	982	Private	$7,859
Park University	15%	MO	970	4,897	Private	$7,998
Portland State University	15%	OR	1,040	13,164	Public	$7,913
Prairie View A & M University	13%	TX	915	5,327	Public	$6,974
Peru State College	13%	NE	N/A	1,248	Public	$5,589
Paine College	13%	GA	830	783	Private	$11,356
Philander Smith College	5%	AR	745	708	Private	$5,886
Purdue University-Calumet Campus	4%	IN	905	6,139	Public	$6,485
Paul Quinn College	4%	TX	1,178	749	Private	$5,407
Peirce College	N/A	PA	N/A	1,207	Private	$8,599
Queens University of Charlotte	50%	NC	1,035	1,218	Private	$13,594
Quincy University	35%	IL	1,030	976	Private	$8,213
Quinnipiac University	64%	CT	1,115	5,426	Private	$12,493
Radford University	35%	VA	1,005	8,179	Public	$6,040
Ramapo College of New Jersey	44%	NJ	1,130	4,593	Public	$8,772
Randolph-Macon College	53%	VA	1,095	1,110	Private	$18,433
Randolph-Macon Woman's College	65%	VA	1,175	694	Private	$21,978
Reed College	57%	OR	1,375	1,284	Private	$24,755
Regis College	45%	MA	940	695	Private	$16,115
Regis University	39%	CO	1,085	3,732	Private	$8,861
Reinhardt College	24%	GA	978	924	Private	$9,502
Rensselaer Polytechnic Institute	64%	NY	1,320	4,919	Private	$21,907
Rhode Island College	15%	RI	965	6,032	Public	$7,476
Rhode Island School of Design	78%	RI	1,205	1,878	Private	$22,221
Rhodes College	75%	TN	1,255	1,661	Private	$22,280
Rice University	79%	TX	1,435	3,075	Private	$40,458
Rider University	45%	NJ	1,050	3,868	Private	$14,918
Ringling School of Art and Design	52%	FL	1,050	1,063	Private	$16,299
Ripon College	61%	WI	1,105	962	Private	$12,651
Rivier College	41%	NH	970	1,123	Private	$11,703
Roanoke College	58%	VA	1,120	1,867	Private	$13,712
Robert Morris University	27%	PA	1,010	3,392	Private	$11,142

Name	4yr Grad Rate	State	Median SAT	Size	Sector	Student Related Exp./FTE
Roberts Wesleyan College	48%	NY	1,095	1,313	Private	$12,218
Rochester College	17%	MI	990	797	Private	$11,377
Rochester Institute of Technology	22%	NY	1,195	11,136	Private	$17,186
Rockford College	33%	IL	1,145	778	Private	$9,909
Rockhurst University	51%	MO	1,145	1,538	Private	$13,149
Rocky Mountain College	27%	MT	1,025	914	Private	$11,879
Roger Williams University	44%	RI	1,085	3,947	Private	$14,242
Rollins College	59%	FL	1,185	2,635	Private	$15,143
Roosevelt University	20%	IL	990	2,718	Private	$13,751
Rose-Hulman Institute of Technology	71%	IN	1,305	1,769	Private	$24,008
Rosemont College	N/A	PA	985	498	Private	$14,202
Rowan University	42%	NJ	1,120	7,685	Public	$10,199
Russell Sage College	51%	NY	1,090	785	Private	N/A
Rust College	N/A	MS	N/A	867	Private	$4,998
Rutgers University-Camden	25%	NJ	1,105	3,248	Public	N/A
Rutgers University-New Brunswick/Piscataway	47%	NJ	1,195	25,145	Public	$19,890
Rutgers University-Newark	26%	NJ	1,100	5,445	Public	N/A
Swarthmore College	86%	PA	1,440	1,474	Private	$39,175
Shimer College	83%	IL	N/A	98	Private	$20,058
Stonehill College	82%	MA	1,205	2,317	Private	$14,808
St. Olaf College	80%	MN	1,240	3,023	Private	$18,902
Santa Clara University	79%	CA	1,205	4,563	Private	$19,639
Saint Johns University	78%	MN	1,165	1,855	Private	$17,498
Skidmore College	77%	NY	1,250	2,607	Private	$23,786
Susquehanna University	77%	PA	1,140	1,926	Private	$15,712
Stanford University	77%	CA	1,455	6,535	Private	$67,108
Simons Rock College of Bard	73%	MA	1,250	379	Private	$22,373
Sewanee: The University of the South	72%	TN	1,244	1,417	Private	$25,451
Siena College	72%	NY	1,120	3,149	Private	$13,699
San Francisco Conservatory of Music	71%	CA	N/A	174	Private	$21,757
St Lawrence University	71%	NY	1,150	2,118	Private	$23,399
Syracuse University	71%	NY	1,215	12,387	Private	$19,551
Saint Michaels College	70%	VT	1,135	1,965	Private	$15,116
St Mary's College of Maryland	70%	MD	1,250	1,887	Public	$11,517
Sarah Lawrence College	70%	NY	N/A	1,290	Private	$25,199
Saint Josephs College-Main Campus	68%	NY	975	846	Private	$39,114
Saint Joseph's University	68%	PA	1,150	4,546	Private	$13,239
Saint Mary's College	68%	IN	1,145	1,376	Private	$22,369

Name	4yr Grad Rate	State	Median SAT	Size	Sector	Student Related Exp./FTE
Saint Anselm College	67%	NH	1,110	1,953	Private	$15,388
Saint Norbert College	66%	WI	1,105	1,944	Private	$11,872
Southwestern University	65%	TX	1,232	1,294	Private	$21,361
Saint Vincent College	64%	PA	1,070	1,506	Private	$11,851
Saint Louis University-Main Campus	63%	MO	1,205	7,730	Private	$16,997
St John's College - Maryland	63%	MD	1,345	473	Private	$22,496
SUNY College at Geneseo	62%	NY	1,270	5,218	Public	$6,469
Simpson College	61%	IA	1,125	1,661	Private	$12,090
SUNY at Binghamton	61%	NY	1,265	10,881	Public	$8,552
Saint Marys College of California	59%	CA	1,090	2,773	Private	$18,250
Southern Methodist University	58%	TX	1,230	6,247	Private	$18,998
Sacred Heart University	57%	CT	1,065	3,531	Private	$12,155
Spring Hill College	56%	AL	1,085	1,216	Private	$12,077
Saint Josephs College - Maine	56%	ME	1,000	1,436	Private	$7,045
Samford University	55%	AL	1,145	2,808	Private	$16,303
Saint John Fisher College	54%	NY	1,085	2,531	Private	$8,709
Salve Regina University	54%	RI	1,080	2,026	Private	$11,732
Saint Mary's University of Minnesota	53%	MN	1,025	1,417	Private	$10,592
Stephens College	53%	MO	1,085	634	Private	$14,552
Saint Bonaventure University	53%	NY	1,045	2,064	Private	$12,874
Stetson University	53%	FL	1,137	2,185	Private	$15,353
Salisbury University	52%	MD	1,130	6,011	Public	$6,367
SUNY at Albany	51%	NY	1,130	11,478	Public	$9,696
Seattle University	51%	WA	1,150	3,979	Private	$15,898
Saint Josephs College - Indiana	49%	IN	990	925	Private	$13,460
SUNY at Fredonia	48%	NY	1,120	4,910	Public	$7,370
Springfield College	48%	MA	1,025	3,177	Private	$10,893
Saint Josephs College-Suffolk Campus	48%	NY	1,050	3,240	Private	N/A
Seattle Pacific University	48%	WA	1,165	2,927	Private	$13,898
Saint Joseph College	46%	CT	1,111	967	Private	$12,217
Saint Francis University	45%	PA	1,050	1,324	Private	$12,690
Shippensburg University of Pennsylvania	45%	PA	1,050	6,270	Public	$7,825
St Francis College	44%	NY	945	2,125	Private	$8,817
Savannah College of Art and Design	44%	GA	1,075	5,731	Private	$13,259
Simpson University	42%	CA	995	905	Private	$10,755
Seton Hill University	42%	PA	N/A	1,326	Private	$9,989
St John's College - New	42%	NM	N/A	432	Private	$20,421

Name	4yr Grad Rate	State	Median SAT	Size	Sector	Student Related Exp./FTE
Mexico						
Seton Hall University	41%	NJ	1,115	4,979	Private	$17,213
SUNY College of Environmental Science and Forestry	40%	NY	1,135	1,431	Public	$14,434
School of the Art Institute of Chicago	40%	IL	1,120	1,959	Private	$17,229
Saint Thomas Aquinas College	39%	NY	940	1,547	Private	$8,504
St. John's University-New York	39%	NY	1,045	12,934	Private	$12,065
Stony Brook University	38%	NY	1,180	13,549	Public	$14,478
Spring Arbor University	38%	MI	1,025	2,145	Private	$8,133
Suffolk University	38%	MA	1,025	4,311	Private	$16,033
Sterling College (KS)	37%	KS	1,025	461	Private	$11,524
SUNY Maritime College	37%	NY	1,095	1,121	Public	$11,145
SUNY at Buffalo	36%	NY	1,160	17,329	Public	$12,689
SUNY College at Oneonta	36%	NY	1,110	5,541	Public	$6,373
Stevens Institute of Technology	36%	NJ	1,275	1,789	Private	$18,859
Southern Wesleyan University	36%	SC	1,013	1,938	Private	$5,043
Southwest Baptist University	36%	MO	1,065	2,086	Private	$7,584
Shorter College	35%	GA	1,025	2,448	Private	$5,489
SUNY College at Purchase	34%	NY	1,095	3,373	Public	$10,171
Saint Peters College	34%	NJ	945	1,952	Private	$13,183
Southwestern College	34%	KS	1,045	800	Private	$13,933
Southern New Hampshire University	33%	NH	995	3,420	Private	$8,620
SUNY College at New Paltz	32%	NY	1,123	5,949	Public	$7,835
SUNY College at Oswego	32%	NY	1,090	6,793	Public	$6,648
SUNY College at Brockport	32%	NY	1,075	6,440	Public	$8,137
Saint Xavier University	32%	IL	1,045	2,655	Private	$11,182
SUNY College at Cortland	32%	NY	1,055	5,776	Public	$6,695
St Marys University	31%	TX	1,048	2,252	Private	$13,048
Southern Vermont College	31%	VT	910	344	Private	$8,013
SUNY College at Plattsburgh	30%	NY	1,030	5,147	Public	$7,731
Saint Leo University	30%	FL	1,005	8,867	Private	$5,943
South Carolina State University	30%	SC	850	3,669	Public	$10,257
Saint Edward's University	30%	TX	1,110	3,319	Private	$12,603
Southern Nazarene University	30%	OK	N/A	1,704	Private	$10,727
Shenandoah University	29%	VA	1,025	1,555	Private	$15,336
SUNY-Potsdam	28%	NY	1,065	3,516	Public	$8,272
Slippery Rock University of Pennsylvania	28%	PA	975	7,060	Public	$7,887
San Francisco Art Institute	27%	CA	1,035	344	Private	$19,276

Name	4yr Grad Rate	State	Median SAT	Size	Sector	Student Related Exp./FTE
Silver Lake College	27%	WI	950	352	Private	$9,680
Schreiner University	27%	TX	960	720	Private	$11,590
Southeast Missouri State University	26%	MO	1,025	7,519	Public	$6,848
SUNY Empire State College	25%	NY	N/A	5,300	Public	$9,070
Southeastern University (FL)	24%	FL	N/A	2,215	Private	$6,481
St Andrews Presbyterian College	24%	NC	1,000	729	Private	$14,132
South Dakota State University	24%	SD	1,045	8,364	Public	$7,280
Sonoma State University	22%	CA	1,045	6,016	Public	$7,184
Siena Heights University	22%	MI	910	1,227	Private	$8,978
Southern Illinois University Edwardsville	22%	IL	1,045	9,803	Public	$9,220
Saint Thomas University	21%	FL	899	1,117	Private	$12,285
Southern Utah University	21%	UT	990	5,221	Public	$5,751
Southern Illinois University Carbondale	21%	IL	1,010	15,540	Public	$13,876
Sterling College (VT)	21%	VT	N/A	93	Private	$13,388
Southwest Minnesota State University	20%	MN	990	3,491	Public	$6,603
Saint Gregorys University	20%	OK	910	616	Private	$5,257
Southwestern Adventist University	20%	TX	980	783	Private	$10,137
Saint Cloud State University	19%	MN	1,010	12,523	Public	$7,034
Sam Houston State University	19%	TX	1,000	12,020	Public	$5,089
Southern Oregon University	19%	OR	1,025	3,740	Public	$7,260
Southeastern University (DC)	19%	DC	N/A	346	Private	$7,877
Shepherd University	18%	WV	970	3,236	Public	$3,967
Southern Adventist University	18%	TN	1,010	2,185	Private	$10,985
San Diego State University	17%	CA	1,080	23,088	Public	$8,288
Spalding University	17%	KY	910	730	Private	$8,196
Saint Augustines College	17%	NC	835	1,135	Private	$11,997
Southern Arkansas University Main Campus	17%	AR	970	2,564	Public	$6,460
Southwestern Oklahoma State University	17%	OK	990	3,993	Public	$5,180
Stephen F Austin State University	17%	TX	1,000	8,972	Public	$6,865
Sheldon Jackson College	15%	AK	N/A	126	Private	$16,171
SUNY College at Old Westbury	15%	NY	945	2,936	Public	$6,680
SUNY College at Buffalo	15%	NY	970	8,215	Public	$9,286
Shawnee State University	14%	OH	N/A	3,405	Public	$5,979
Salem State College	14%	MA	945	6,077	Public	$8,357
SUNY College of Technology at Alfred	13%	NY	980	3,121	Public	$6,240

Name	4yr Grad Rate	State	Median SAT	Size	Sector	Student Related Exp./FTE
Sojourner-Douglass College	13%	MD	N/A	718	Private	$6,107
San Francisco State University	11%	CA	1,010	19,970	Public	$7,714
South Dakota School of Mines and Technology	11%	SD	1,125	1,747	Public	$8,102
Shaw University	11%	NC	765	2,377	Private	$8,700
Southeastern Oklahoma State University	11%	OK	970	3,171	Public	$6,026
Southern Connecticut State University	11%	CT	950	7,234	Public	$9,047
Savannah State University	10%	GA	900	2,575	Public	$7,175
Stillman College	9%	AL	825	783	Private	$9,300
Southeastern Louisiana University	8%	LA	950	12,548	Public	$5,029
Sierra Nevada College	8%	NV	1,012	348	Private	$11,670
San Jose State University	7%	CA	1,010	18,878	Public	$7,897
Saginaw Valley State University	7%	MI	990	6,674	Public	$6,033
Southern Polytechnic State University	6%	GA	1,110	2,572	Public	$8,396
San Diego Christian College	6%	CA	985	475	Private	$11,921
Sul Ross State University	5%	TX	N/A	1,715	Public	$7,908
Southern University and A & M College	0%	LA	845	8,278	Public	$7,682
Southern Christian University	N/A	AL	N/A	330	Private	$6,423
Samuel Merritt College	N/A	CA	N/A	324	Private	$18,932
Scripps College	N/A	CA	1,355	882	Private	$36,540
Spelman College	N/A	GA	1,060	2,255	Private	$16,590
Saint Mary-of-the-Woods College	N/A	IN	1,015	882	Private	$10,168
Saint Ambrose University	N/A	IA	1,010	2,366	Private	$9,532
Southern University at New Orleans	N/A	LA	N/A	N/A	Public	N/A
Simmons College	N/A	MA	1,105	1,780	Private	$18,833
Smith College	N/A	MA	1,265	2,622	Private	$32,932
SUNY College of Agriculture and Technology at Cobleskill	N/A	NY	925	2,401	Public	$6,654
SUNY Institute of Technology at Utica-Rome	N/A	NY	1,122	1,500	Public	$10,683
Salem College	N/A	NC	1,100	757	Private	$13,831
Sinte Gleska University	N/A	SD	N/A	631	Private	$8,080
Saint Pauls College	N/A	VA	765	699	Private	$6,483
Sweet Briar College	N/A	VA	1,130	715	Private	$27,016
Saint Martin's University	N/A	WA	1,025	1,057	Private	$10,066
Tufts University	87%	MA	1,405	5,764	Private	$27,599
Thomas Aquinas College	82%	CA	1,296	359	Private	$10,836

Name	4yr Grad Rate	State	Median SAT	Size	Sector	Student Related Exp./FTE
Thomas More College of Liberal Arts	81%	NH	N/A	84	Private	$5,797
Trinity College	80%	CT	1,310	2,168	Private	$31,754
Taylor University-Upland	69%	IN	1,165	1,814	Private	$13,970
The Juilliard School	68%	NY	N/A	545	Private	$40,279
Transylvania University	67%	KY	1,165	1,140	Private	$15,544
Trinity University - Texas	67%	TX	1,295	2,429	Private	$19,718
The College of New Jersey	66%	NJ	1,270	5,782	Public	$9,827
The College of Wooster	66%	OH	1,225	1,824	Private	$19,111
Tulane University of Louisiana	60%	LA	1,350	N/A	Private	$19,951
The New England Conservatory of Music	58%	MA	801	396	Private	$26,474
The University of the Arts	55%	PA	1,055	2,050	Private	$16,589
The College of Saint Scholastica	55%	MN	1,085	2,402	Private	$11,545
Trinity Christian College	51%	IL	1,025	1,126	Private	$13,101
Trinity International University	49%	IL	1,050	951	Private	$9,901
Thomas College	47%	ME	930	642	Private	$6,730
The Boston Conservatory	47%	MA	N/A	402	Private	$16,474
The University of Texas at Austin	46%	TX	1,235	34,747	Public	$11,344
The Master's College and Seminary	45%	CA	1,145	1,026	Private	$14,519
Touro College	45%	NY	N/A	10,298	Private	$7,605
Texas Christian University	45%	TX	1,165	6,869	Private	$15,470
The New School	45%	NY	1,125	4,981	Private	$14,717
The College of Saint Rose	45%	NY	1,065	2,889	Private	$10,461
The University of Tampa	44%	FL	1,080	4,313	Private	$9,052
The Evergreen State College	44%	WA	1,130	3,827	Public	$7,244
Tabor College	44%	KS	1,025	521	Private	$10,509
The Richard Stockton College of New Jersey	41%	NJ	1,115	5,957	Public	$7,641
Truman State University	39%	MO	1,240	5,493	Public	$8,638
The University of Findlay	38%	OH	1,045	2,966	Private	$10,089
Texas Lutheran University	38%	TX	1,050	1,364	Private	$9,412
Texas A & M University	37%	TX	1,200	34,179	Public	$10,044
Trevecca Nazarene University	36%	TN	1,045	1,073	Private	$8,271
The University of Alabama	36%	AL	1,065	16,405	Public	$9,157
Tri-State University	34%	IN	1,055	1,056	Private	$9,917
Towson University	32%	MD	1,090	13,373	Public	$6,862
The University of Texas at Dallas	31%	TX	1,245	7,546	Public	$9,175
Thomas More College	31%	KY	1,010	1,200	Private	$9,378
Troy University	31%	AL	950	11,856	Public	$5,743

Name	4yr Grad Rate	State	Median SAT	Size	Sector	Student Related Exp./FTE
The University of Tennessee	31%	TN	1,125	19,255	Public	$18,232
Toccoa Falls College	30%	GA	1,020	883	Private	$7,475
Tougaloo College	30%	MS	865	907	Private	$9,605
Temple University	30%	PA	1,090	22,022	Public	$15,868
The University of Virginia's College at Wise	27%	VA	980	1,622	Public	$6,640
Tusculum College	27%	TN	970	2,255	Private	$5,516
Tennessee Wesleyan College	26%	TN	970	777	Private	$7,643
Tuskegee University	25%	AL	890	2,431	Private	$12,967
The University of Tennessee-Chattanooga	25%	TN	990	6,552	Public	$7,682
Texas Tech University	25%	TX	1,130	21,548	Public	$8,059
Tennessee State University	22%	TN	865	6,261	Public	$10,566
Tiffin University	21%	OH	950	1,144	Private	$7,225
Texas Woman's University	21%	TX	965	5,125	Public	$8,796
The College of New Rochelle	21%	NY	970	4,914	Private	$6,393
Tarleton State University	21%	TX	975	6,527	Public	$5,498
The University of Tennessee-Martin	21%	TN	1,010	5,323	Public	$7,527
Trinity Washington University	21%	DC	N/A	681	Private	$10,599
Texas State University-San Marcos	21%	TX	1,060	19,977	Public	$5,414
Texas A & M University-Corpus Christi	20%	TX	932	5,857	Public	$7,136
The University of Montana	20%	MT	1,045	10,286	Public	$7,120
The University of West Florida	19%	FL	1,085	6,571	Public	$8,268
Tennessee Technological University	19%	TN	1,065	6,720	Public	$7,496
Talladega College	18%	AL	905	349	Private	$11,581
Texas A & M University-Commerce	17%	TX	985	4,311	Public	$7,242
The University of Texas at Arlington	14%	TX	1,060	15,880	Public	$6,869
Texas A & M University at Galveston	14%	TX	1,081	1,537	Public	$7,878
The University of Texas-Pan American	11%	TX	865	12,059	Public	$6,456
Texas A & M University-Kingsville	10%	TX	885	4,174	Public	$7,505
The University of Texas at San Antonio	7%	TX	995	19,513	Public	$5,396
The University of Texas at El Paso	4%	TX	N/A	12,662	Public	$6,322
The University of Montana-Western	3%	MT	N/A	1,014	Public	$7,731
Texas Southern University	3%	TX	N/A	8,413	Public	$6,778

Name	4yr Grad Rate	State	Median SAT	Size	Sector	Student Related Exp./FTE
Texas Wesleyan University	2%	TX	1,094	1,115	Private	$13,092
Thomas University	N/A	GA	N/A	568	Private	$7,167
Trinity College of Nursing and Health Sciences	N/A	IL	N/A	131	Private	$19,994
Thomas Edison State College	N/A	NJ	N/A	3,635	Public	$623
Thiel College	N/A	PA	960	1,285	Private	$11,037
University of Notre Dame	90%	IN	1,385	8,265	Private	$24,342
University of Pennsylvania	88%	PA	1,430	10,979	Private	$54,537
United States Naval Academy	87%	MD	1,285	4,422	Public	$56,418
United States Military Academy	84%	NY	1,265	N/A	Public	$35,896
University of Virginia-Main Campus	83%	VA	1,325	13,668	Public	$14,179
University of Chicago	82%	IL	1,440	4,633	Private	$60,875
University of Richmond	79%	VA	1,315	3,285	Private	$21,668
Union College - New York	79%	NY	1,255	2,223	Private	$23,923
United States Air Force Academy	77%	CO	1,320	4,463	Public	$43,969
Ursinus College	76%	PA	1,220	1,558	Private	$18,760
University of Scranton	75%	PA	1,140	3,933	Private	$13,746
University of North Carolina at Chapel Hill	71%	NC	1,290	16,195	Public	$27,108
University of Mary Washington	71%	VA	1,225	3,708	Public	$7,290
University of Rochester	71%	NY	1,320	4,522	Private	$39,643
University of Michigan-Ann Arbor	70%	MI	1,280	24,786	Public	$19,524
University of Puget Sound	68%	WA	1,230	2,580	Private	$19,379
United States Coast Guard Academy	65%	CT	1,290	1,005	Public	$47,317
University of Southern California	65%	CA	1,355	16,347	Private	$29,167
University of San Diego	64%	CA	1,180	4,857	Private	$17,476
University of California-Berkeley	61%	CA	1,330	22,691	Public	$18,854
University of Illinois at Urbana-Champaign	61%	IL	1,260	30,244	Public	$10,579
University of Delaware	60%	DE	1,205	16,152	Public	$16,268
University of Dallas	60%	TX	1,235	1,102	Private	$14,913
University of Dayton	60%	OH	1,165	7,084	Private	$12,585
University of California-Los Angeles	59%	CA	1,295	24,172	Public	$30,051
United States Merchant Marine Academy	59%	NY	1,235	927	Public	$25,546
University of Miami	58%	FL	1,260	10,023	Private	$26,289
University of Portland	58%	OR	1,180	2,869	Private	$11,525
University of Denver	57%	CO	1,165	4,580	Private	$17,879

Name	4yr Grad Rate	State	Median SAT	Size	Sector	Student Related Exp./FTE
University of Judaism	56%	CA	1,100	125	Private	$19,071
University of St Thomas - Minnesota	55%	MN	1,125	5,289	Private	$16,172
University of New Hampshire-Main Campus	55%	NH	1,130	11,112	Public	$10,545
University of Maryland-College Park	55%	MD	1,275	23,989	Public	$12,652
University of Redlands	54%	CA	1,170	3,071	Private	$12,109
University of Florida	54%	FL	1,260	32,837	Public	$12,936
University of New England	54%	ME	1,045	1,591	Private	$14,340
University of Connecticut	53%	CT	1,185	15,568	Public	$15,293
University of California-San Diego	53%	CA	1,260	19,944	Public	$19,790
University of Vermont	52%	VT	1,165	9,054	Public	$14,677
University of Pittsburgh-Main Campus	52%	PA	1,235	15,741	Public	$20,526
University of California-Irvine	51%	CA	1,200	19,532	Public	$19,204
University of San Francisco	48%	CA	1,125	5,087	Private	$17,564
University of Massachusetts-Amherst	48%	MA	1,140	18,501	Public	$12,884
University of California-Santa Cruz	48%	CA	1,165	13,301	Public	$10,783
University of Washington-Seattle Campus	48%	WA	1,200	24,540	Public	$21,893
University of California-Santa Barbara	47%	CA	1,180	17,647	Public	$11,540
University of Tulsa	46%	OK	1,205	2,689	Private	$18,837
University of Georgia	45%	GA	1,225	23,555	Public	$8,091
University of the Pacific	45%	CA	1,190	3,390	Private	$20,261
University of Wisconsin-Madison	44%	WI	1,260	27,869	Public	$13,439
Union University	44%	TN	1,105	1,767	Private	$10,526
University of North Carolina-Wilmington	43%	NC	1,125	10,046	Public	$6,978
University of California-Davis	43%	CA	1,180	21,341	Public	$20,225
University of Evansville	43%	IN	1,145	2,457	Private	$14,850
University of Saint Mary	42%	KS	930	427	Private	$10,091
University of Hartford	41%	CT	1,065	4,969	Private	$14,138
University of Mary	41%	ND	1,045	2,095	Private	$5,041
University of South Carolina-Columbia	40%	SC	1,150	17,053	Public	$11,074
University of Minnesota-Morris	40%	MN	1,125	1,581	Public	$10,343
University of Rhode Island	40%	RI	1,085	10,359	Public	$10,273
University of Missouri-Columbia	40%	MO	1,165	20,422	Public	$10,104
University of Iowa	40%	IA	1,125	18,896	Public	$12,911

Name	4yr Grad Rate	State	Median SAT	Size	Sector	Student Related Exp./FTE
University of Oregon	39%	OR	1,115	15,488	Public	$9,222
University of Colorado at Boulder	38%	CO	1,165	24,585	Public	$10,655
University of St Francis	38%	IL	990	1,548	Private	$8,984
University of Indianapolis	37%	IN	1,030	2,704	Private	$15,464
University of Maine at Farmington	37%	ME	1,015	2,233	Public	$8,370
University of Sioux Falls	37%	SD	1,025	1,105	Private	$8,006
University of California-Riverside	37%	CA	1,075	14,036	Public	$9,722
University of Pittsburgh-Johnstown	37%	PA	1,035	3,001	Public	$6,806
University of Charleston	35%	WV	1,025	897	Private	$10,944
University of Northern Iowa	34%	IA	1,045	10,167	Public	$7,450
University of Maine	34%	ME	1,075	8,138	Public	$9,991
University of Mississippi Main Campus	33%	MS	1,065	11,494	Public	$8,671
University of Bridgeport	33%	CT	890	1,390	Private	$10,156
Upper Iowa University	33%	IA	930	3,125	Private	$6,372
University of Minnesota-Twin Cities	33%	MN	1,165	28,910	Public	$17,013
University of La Verne	32%	CA	1,006	3,223	Private	$12,240
University of the Ozarks	31%	AR	1,025	601	Private	$15,811
Utica College	31%	NY	975	2,158	Private	$12,296
University of Kansas Main Campus	31%	KS	1,105	19,315	Public	$10,396
University of North Carolina at Asheville	31%	NC	1,165	3,034	Public	$7,977
University of Central Florida	30%	FL	1,140	31,717	Public	$6,278
University of Kentucky	30%	KY	1,105	17,601	Public	$12,182
University of Massachusetts-Lowell	30%	MA	1,188	6,566	Public	$11,252
Union Institute & University	30%	OH	N/A	823	Private	$9,917
University of North Carolina at Greensboro	30%	NC	1,040	11,186	Public	$9,509
University of Arizona	30%	AZ	1,125	25,971	Public	$10,251
University of Arkansas Main Campus	30%	AR	1,145	12,589	Public	$8,618
University of Northern Colorado	29%	CO	1,010	10,338	Public	$6,297
Union College - Nebraska	29%	NE	1,025	800	Private	$11,380
University of Massachusetts-Dartmouth	28%	MA	1,055	6,806	Public	$9,206
Unity College	28%	ME	1,010	521	Private	$10,728
University of Maryland-Baltimore County	28%	MD	1,215	8,455	Public	$9,833

Name	4yr Grad Rate	State	Median SAT	Size	Sector	Student Related Exp./FTE
University of Mobile	27%	AL	1,045	1,365	Private	$7,125
Ursuline College	27%	OH	970	887	Private	$12,397
University of Pittsburgh-Greensburg	27%	PA	1,060	1,693	Public	$6,227
University of Detroit Mercy	27%	MI	1,065	2,401	Private	$17,049
University of Wisconsin-La Crosse	26%	WI	1,145	7,888	Public	$7,744
University of North Carolina at Charlotte	26%	NC	1,070	14,612	Public	$8,726
University of Wyoming	26%	WY	1,065	8,303	Public	$11,185
University of Saint Francis-Ft Wayne	25%	IN	980	1,485	Private	$10,442
University of New Haven	25%	CT	1,040	2,463	Private	$13,953
University of Mary Hardin-Baylor	25%	TX	1,040	2,385	Private	$9,435
University of Pittsburgh-Bradford	25%	PA	1,005	1,113	Public	$10,310
University of Minnesota-Duluth	24%	MN	1,065	8,885	Public	$6,479
University of Southern Mississippi	24%	MS	970	11,307	Public	$7,205
University of Oklahoma Norman Campus	24%	OK	1,165	18,471	Public	$7,962
University of St Thomas - Texas	24%	TX	1,165	1,522	Private	$10,333
University of Wisconsin-River Falls	24%	WI	1,010	5,417	Public	$7,756
University of Dubuque	23%	IA	930	1,142	Private	$10,615
University of Wisconsin-Green Bay	23%	WI	1,045	4,799	Public	$7,083
University of Nebraska at Lincoln	23%	NE	1,145	16,191	Public	$8,995
University of South Dakota	23%	SD	1,045	4,985	Public	$10,480
University of Colorado at Colorado Springs	23%	CO	1,065	5,413	Public	$6,449
Utah State University	22%	UT	1,105	11,398	Public	$8,116
University of Wisconsin-Stevens Point	22%	WI	1,045	7,967	Public	$7,887
University of Montevallo	22%	AL	1,010	2,443	Public	$7,868
Union College - Kentucky	22%	KY	910	542	Private	$9,553
Urbana University	22%	OH	930	1,090	Private	$8,918
University of South Florida	22%	FL	1,120	27,198	Public	$9,441
University of North Dakota	22%	ND	1,025	9,741	Public	$12,222
University of South Carolina-Aiken	21%	SC	990	2,563	Public	$7,354
University of Illinois at Chicago	21%	IL	1,065	14,205	Public	$18,891

Name	4yr Grad Rate	State	Median SAT	Size	Sector	Student Related Exp./FTE
University of Missouri-Rolla	21%	MO	1,225	4,032	Public	$13,271
University of Utah	21%	UT	1,085	18,419	Public	$11,736
University of Wisconsin-Whitewater	21%	WI	1,030	8,844	Public	$7,092
University of the Cumberlands	20%	KY	1,010	1,485	Private	$9,812
University of North Florida	20%	FL	1,110	10,829	Public	$6,260
University of Missouri-St Louis	20%	MO	1,065	8,127	Public	$9,870
University of North Carolina at Pembroke	20%	NC	940	4,122	Public	$8,724
University of Central Arkansas	20%	AR	1,085	9,408	Public	$5,860
University of Maryland-University College	20%	MD	N/A	8,187	Public	$11,147
University of Idaho	20%	ID	1,065	8,754	Public	$7,865
University of the Incarnate Word	20%	TX	970	3,022	Private	$10,499
University of Wisconsin-Eau Claire	19%	WI	1,105	9,636	Public	$7,721
University of Cincinnati-Main Campus	19%	OH	1,065	17,236	Public	$13,431
University of Maryland-Eastern Shore	19%	MD	835	3,255	Public	$10,329
University of North Texas	18%	TX	1,100	21,646	Public	$8,038
University of Memphis	18%	TN	990	12,967	Public	$9,598
University of South Carolina-Upstate	18%	SC	1,015	3,846	Public	$6,587
University of North Alabama	17%	AL	970	4,768	Public	$5,947
University of Missouri-Kansas City	17%	MO	1,105	6,948	Public	$14,337
University of Maine at Machias	17%	ME	970	691	Public	$6,956
University of Toledo	17%	OH	1,030	14,071	Public	$9,998
University of Minnesota-Crookston	17%	MN	990	1,355	Public	$6,490
University of South Alabama	16%	AL	990	8,378	Public	$10,197
University of Michigan-Dearborn	16%	MI	1,085	4,817	Public	$9,996
University of Nebraska at Kearney	16%	NE	1,010	5,057	Public	$6,958
University of Massachusetts-Boston	15%	MA	1,005	6,831	Public	$14,108
University of Nevada-Reno	15%	NV	1,060	11,150	Public	$14,586
University of Wisconsin-Stout	15%	WI	990	6,938	Public	$8,675
University of Alabama in Huntsville	15%	AL	1,145	4,631	Public	$8,731
University of Wisconsin-Milwaukee	15%	WI	1,030	20,209	Public	$9,100
University of Southern Indiana	15%	IN	950	8,069	Public	$5,182
University of Wisconsin-	15%	WI	1,030	9,112	Public	$7,661

Name	4yr Grad Rate	State	Median SAT	Size	Sector	Student Related Exp./FTE
Oshkosh						
University of Wisconsin-Superior	14%	WI	1,045	2,283	Public	$8,615
University of Louisville	14%	KY	1,085	12,605	Public	$13,656
University of Maine at Presque Isle	14%	ME	N/A	1,257	Public	$5,971
University of Science and Arts of Oklahoma	14%	OK	1,005	1,186	Public	$5,576
University of Alabama at Birmingham	14%	AL	1,065	9,196	Public	$20,681
University of Colorado at Denver and Health Sciences Center	14%	CO	1,025	7,396	Public	$22,609
University of Louisiana at Lafayette	14%	LA	895	13,805	Public	$4,435
University of Wisconsin-Platteville	14%	WI	1,045	5,408	Public	$8,203
University of the Sciences in Philadelphia	13%	PA	1,140	1,479	Private	$16,762
University of Akron Main Campus	13%	OH	990	14,137	Public	$8,317
University of Central Oklahoma	12%	OK	990	11,528	Public	$5,269
University of New Mexico-Main Campus	12%	NM	1,010	16,134	Public	$9,828
University of Houston	12%	TX	1,070	22,640	Public	$8,031
University of Great Falls	12%	MT	N/A	548	Private	$10,971
University of West Alabama	12%	AL	885	1,595	Public	$8,838
University of West Georgia	11%	GA	1,020	7,396	Public	$6,140
University of Nevada-Las Vegas	11%	NV	1,015	17,919	Public	$8,650
University of Hawaii at Manoa	11%	HI	1,105	12,689	Public	$14,194
University of Michigan-Flint	11%	MI	1,010	4,196	Public	$7,937
University of Wisconsin-Parkside	11%	WI	950	3,970	Public	$7,898
University of Arkansas at Monticello	11%	AR	N/A	2,427	Public	$6,163
University of Hawaii at Hilo	11%	HI	980	2,823	Public	$10,595
University of Nebraska at Omaha	10%	NE	1,045	9,464	Public	$7,247
University of Louisiana at Monroe	10%	LA	970	6,965	Public	$5,436
University of Southern Maine	10%	ME	1,005	6,066	Public	$9,539
University of Rio Grande	10%	OH	N/A	1,844	Private	$7,063
University of Alaska Fairbanks	9%	AK	1,045	4,686	Public	$14,546
University of Arkansas at Little Rock	9%	AR	N/A	6,949	Public	$7,539

Name	4yr Grad Rate	State	Median SAT	Size	Sector	Student Related Exp./FTE
University of Alaska Anchorage	8%	AK	1,020	9,809	Public	$9,660
University of Maine at Fort Kent	7%	ME	889	906	Public	$6,820
University of Arkansas at Pine Bluff	7%	AR	775	2,931	Public	$6,035
University of New Orleans	7%	LA	990	2,916	Public	$6,867
University of Alaska Southeast	6%	AK	1,060	1,548	Public	$13,103
University of the District of Columbia	5%	DC	N/A	3,034	Public	$17,942
University of Houston-Downtown	2%	TX	N/A	7,722	Public	$5,137
University of Maine at Augusta	0%	ME	N/A	2,852	Public	$5,727
Valdosta State University	18%	GA	1,015	8,069	Public	$6,250
Valley City State University	21%	ND	970	860	Public	$8,271
Valparaiso University	64%	IN	1,165	2,871	Private	$14,595
Vanderbilt University	83%	TN	1,370	6,329	Private	$53,702
Vandercook College of Music	63%	IL	1,025	120	Private	$17,975
Vanguard University of Southern California	38%	CA	1,005	1,632	Private	$10,535
Vassar College	85%	NY	1,385	2,343	Private	$34,511
Vaughn College of Aeronautics and Technology	10%	NY	1,030	937	Private	$13,216
Vermont Technical College	N/A	VT	980	1,111	Public	$13,224
Villa Julie College	52%	MD	1,010	2,465	Private	$10,631
Villanova University	82%	PA	1,265	6,717	Private	$19,193
Virginia Commonwealth University	20%	VA	1,060	17,414	Public	$11,757
Virginia Intermont College	92%	VA	905	730	Private	$5,760
Virginia Military Institute	59%	VA	1,150	1,369	Public	$17,212
Virginia Polytechnic Institute and State University	52%	VA	1,200	21,267	Public	$9,333
Virginia State University	21%	VA	835	4,151	Public	$8,012
Virginia Union University	15%	VA	N/A	1,321	Private	$7,859
Virginia Wesleyan College	37%	VA	1,010	1,211	Private	$13,013
Viterbo University	30%	WI	1,010	1,574	Private	$10,754
Voorhees College	40%	SC	775	696	Private	$10,648
Wabash College	74%	IN	1,195	873	Private	$28,733
Wagner College	54%	NY	1,165	1,915	Private	$11,658
Wake Forest University	79%	NC	1,325	4,180	Private	$63,557
Walla Walla College	18%	WA	1,045	1,575	Private	$12,104
Walsh University	39%	OH	1,010	1,573	Private	$8,322
Warner Pacific College	36%	OR	1,018	555	Private	$11,661
Warner Southern College	20%	FL	945	826	Private	$7,358
Warren Wilson College	39%	NC	1,175	824	Private	$14,604

Name	4yr Grad Rate	State	Median SAT	Size	Sector	Student Related Exp./FTE
Wartburg College	57%	IA	1,085	1,758	Private	$12,830
Washburn University	20%	KS	1,010	4,909	Public	$7,434
Washington & Jefferson College	64%	PA	1,140	1,406	Private	$16,743
Washington and Lee University	85%	VA	1,385	1,767	Private	$28,988
Washington College	68%	MD	1,150	1,322	Private	$16,190
Washington State University	33%	WA	1,105	17,719	Public	$9,500
Washington University in St Louis	83%	MO	1,440	6,601	Private	$81,826
Wayland Baptist University	14%	TX	985	2,429	Private	$10,010
Wayne State College	27%	NE	990	2,557	Public	$7,045
Wayne State University	13%	MI	945	14,862	Public	$13,321
Waynesburg College	45%	PA	965	1,433	Private	$10,543
Webb Institute	75%	NY	1,415	80	Private	$47,112
Webber International University	35%	FL	905	523	Private	$8,043
Weber State University	11%	UT	1,030	12,746	Public	$5,748
Webster University	41%	MO	1,105	3,044	Private	$9,686
Wellesley College	N/A	MA	1,395	2,254	Private	$38,129
Wells College	N/A	NY	1,105	409	Private	$23,717
Wentworth Institute of Technology	23%	MA	1,073	3,306	Private	$10,282
Wesley College	24%	DE	N/A	1,869	Private	$7,231
Wesleyan College	N/A	GA	1,095	450	Private	$15,695
Wesleyan University	84%	CT	1,400	2,755	Private	$31,006
West Chester University of Pennsylvania	31%	PA	1,050	10,138	Public	$8,061
West Liberty State College	18%	WV	930	2,058	Public	$4,870
West Texas A & M University	14%	TX	1,005	4,914	Public	$5,679
West Virginia State University	5%	WV	865	2,762	Public	$7,644
West Virginia University	26%	WV	1,045	18,803	Public	$7,958
West Virginia University Institute of Technology	18%	WV	1,125	1,190	Public	$6,959
West Virginia Wesleyan College	41%	WV	1,045	1,307	Private	$9,371
Western Carolina University	25%	NC	1,025	6,337	Public	$7,642
Western Connecticut State University	13%	CT	995	4,400	Public	$8,563
Western Illinois University	32%	IL	990	10,639	Public	$8,373
Western Kentucky University	30%	KY	970	14,024	Public	$6,483
Western Michigan University	20%	MI	1,045	19,651	Public	$7,731
Western New England College	50%	MA	1,065	2,522	Private	$13,552
Western New Mexico University	5%	NM	N/A	1,600	Public	$8,194

Name	4yr Grad Rate	State	Median SAT	Size	Sector	Student Related Exp./FTE
Western Oregon University	21%	OR	985	3,979	Public	$6,501
Western State College of Colorado	12%	CO	970	2,113	Public	$6,291
Western Washington University	29%	WA	1,135	12,296	Public	$7,097
Westfield State College	42%	MA	1,025	4,297	Public	$7,354
Westminster College - Missouri	47%	MO	1,125	903	Private	$12,227
Westminster College - Pennsylvania	68%	PA	1,035	1,476	Private	$14,348
Westminster College - Utah	39%	UT	1,085	1,715	Private	$13,751
Westmont College	71%	CA	1,210	1,360	Private	$16,818
Wheaton College - Illinois	78%	IL	1,345	2,367	Private	$19,892
Wheaton College - Massachusetts	71%	MA	1,260	1,562	Private	$23,141
Wheeling Jesuit University	45%	WV	1,125	1,105	Private	$10,344
Wheelock College	52%	MA	985	648	Private	$17,909
Whitman College	80%	WA	1,330	1,491	Private	$21,542
Whittier College	55%	CA	1,065	1,256	Private	$14,563
Whitworth College	60%	WA	1,205	2,103	Private	$11,767
Wichita State University	14%	KS	1,045	8,392	Public	$8,066
Widener University-Main Campus	41%	PA	980	2,583	Private	$25,541
Wilberforce University	11%	OH	765	1,150	Private	$8,662
Wiley College	17%	TX	N/A	791	Private	$6,597
Wilkes University	42%	PA	1,064	2,041	Private	$9,699
Willamette University	66%	OR	1,225	1,867	Private	$18,394
William Carey College	17%	MS	1,025	1,434	Private	$5,090
William Jewell College	48%	MO	1,165	1,386	Private	$14,822
William Paterson University of New Jersey	16%	NJ	1,000	8,018	Public	$8,565
William Penn University	21%	IA	930	1,833	Private	$4,814
William Woods University	34%	MO	1,025	899	Private	$7,686
Williams Baptist College	28%	AR	1,010	533	Private	$4,939
Williams College	92%	MA	1,435	2,019	Private	$45,624
Wilmington College - Delaware	2%	DE	N/A	3,355	Private	$6,938
Wilmington College - Ohio	46%	OH	1,010	1,501	Private	$7,679
Wilson College	51%	PA	1,015	476	Private	$15,021
Wingate University	37%	NC	1,025	1,322	Private	$11,263
Winona State University	27%	MN	1,050	7,012	Public	$6,878
Winston-Salem State University	19%	NC	880	4,842	Public	$9,417
Winthrop University	33%	SC	1,060	4,787	Public	$7,853
Wisconsin Lutheran College	47%	WI	1,125	672	Private	$16,049

Name	4yr Grad Rate	State	Median SAT	Size	Sector	Student Related Exp./FTE
Wittenberg University	63%	OH	1,105	1,979	Private	$16,460
Wofford College	72%	SC	1,208	1,186	Private	$19,917
Woodbury College	N/A	VT	N/A	108	Private	$12,718
Woodbury University	34%	CA	935	1,107	Private	$10,676
Worcester Polytechnic Institute	64%	MA	1,280	2,841	Private	$20,925
Worcester State College	17%	MA	1,005	3,694	Public	$7,453
Wright State University-Main Campus	19%	OH	990	11,056	Public	$11,721
Xavier University	67%	OH	1,165	3,515	Private	$13,743
Xavier University of Louisiana	25%	LA	990	2,248	Private	N/A
Yale University	88%	CT	1,480	5,370	Private	$101,788
Yeshiva University	36%	NY	1,220	2,870	Private	$31,427
York College	22%	NE	1,025	425	Private	$8,874
York College Pennsylvania	41%	PA	1,080	4,781	Private	$6,934
Youngstown State University	13%	OH	950	10,058	Public	$7,283

Appendix C

SAT Optional Universities/Colleges* - This is a sampling from Fairtest.org of several colleges that are SAT-optional, along with a cross reference with U.S. News and World Reports 2009 college rankings.

College	State	4-Yr Grad Rate	6-yr Grad Rate	US News Ranking
Mount Holyoke College	MA	86%	89%	# 27 Best Liberal Arts College
College of Holy Cross	MA	86%	89%	# 35 Best Liberal Arts College
Providence College	RI	85%	87%	# 3 Best Universities - North
Middlebury College	VT	85%	91%	# 5 Best Liberal Arts College
Bowdoin College	ME	83%	88%	# 6 Best Liberal Arts College
Bates College	ME	83%	89%	# 25 Best Liberal Arts College
Stonehill College	MA	82%	85%	# 115 Best Liberal Arts College
Wake Forest University	NC	79%	89%	# 28 Best National Universities
Franklin & Marshall College	PA	79%	84%	# 42 Best Liberal Arts College
Dickinson College	PA	79%	83%	# 45 Best Liberal Arts College
Muhlenberg College	PA	79%	83%	# 71 Best Liberal Arts College
Furman University	SC	79%	83%	# 37 Best Liberal Arts College
Gustavus Adolphus College	MN	78%	86%	# 88 Best Liberal Arts College
Gettysburg College	PA	77%	81%	# 49 Best Liberal Arts College
Denison University	OH	75%	79%	# 53 Best Liberal Arts College
St. Lawrence University	NY	74%	77%	# 58 Best Liberal Arts College
Ursinus College	PA	72%	75%	# 81 Best Liberal Arts College
Augustana College	IL	71%	76%	# 88 Best Liberal Arts College
Beacon College	FL	69%	69%	Best Liberal Arts College 4th Tier
Bard College	NY	67%	76%	# 37 Best Liberal Arts College
Hobart & William Smith College	NY	67%	71%	# 68 Best Liberal Arts College
Nazareth College	NY	67%	77%	# 23 Best Universities - North

Lewis & Clark College	OR	67%	71%	# 71 Best Liberal Arts College
McDaniel College	MD	66%	72%	Best Liberal Arts College 3rd Tier
Drew University	NJ	66%	71%	# 71 Best Liberal Arts College
Kings College	PA	65%	72%	# 35 Best Universities - North
Pitzer College	CA	64%	71%	# 49 Best Liberal Arts College
Lake Forest College	IL	64%	69%	# 94 Best Liberal Arts College
Lawrence University	WI	63%	79%	# 56 Best Liberal Arts College
Russell Sage College	NY	62%	67%	Best Liberal Arts College 3rd Tier
Rollins College	FL	59%	68%	# 1 Best Universities - South
Whitworth University	WA	59%	74%	# 6 Best Universities - West
Goucher College	MD	58%	67%	# 111 Best Liberal Arts College
Wittenberg University	OH	57%	61%	Best Liberal Arts College 3rd Tier
Albright College	PA	53%	60%	Best Liberal Arts College 3rd Tier
Bennington College	VT	50%	57%	# 104 Best Liberal Arts College
Guilford College	NC	49%	58%	Best Liberal Arts College 3rd Tier
Yeshiva University	NY	48%	84%	# 55 Best National Universities
Baldwin-Wallace College	OH	48%	67%	# 12 Best Universities - Midwest
Hartwick College	NY	46%	61%	Best Liberal Arts College 3rd Tier
Salisbury University	MD	45%	68%	# 35 Best Universities - North
Chatham University	PA	42%	47%	# 65 Best Universities - North
Southern Nazarene University	OK	36%	54%	# 53 Best Universities - West
University of Arizona	AZ	33%	56%	# 96 Best National Universities
College of the Atlantic	ME	32%	54%	Best Liberal Arts College 3rd Tier
Kansas State University	KS	25%	58%	# 130 Best National Universities
Green Mountain College	VT	25%	41%	Best Liberal Arts College 4th Tier
University of Wisconsin-Whitwater	WI	20%	53%	# 60 Best Universities - Midwest
Bennett College	NC	19%	35%	Best Liberal Arts College 4th Tier
Humbolt State University	CA	11%	42%	# 49 Best Universities - West
San Francisco State University	CA	11%	44%	# 53 Best Universities - West
Weber State University	UT	5%	40%	# 53 Best Universities - West
Merrimack College	MA	0%	77%	Best Liberal Arts College 3rd Tier

* This listing is for illustrative purposes and should not be used as the sole method to select a college. The author is not responsible for any errors or omissions.

About the Author

Kenneth Albert | M.S. | Certified College Planning Specialist and author of the Right Fit™ Program.

As an independent college consultant, Kenneth Albert has helped hundreds of families understand and take control of the college planning process. He created The Right Fit™ Program to guide students and parents through all aspects of the college application process and know how to avoid the major pitfalls. Ken is a partner with SERVE, a private nonprofit agency founded in 1969 that recruits talented volunteers from the community to serve the Hillsborough County School District. As a volunteer speaker, he serves as a motivator and role model to middle and high school students in the Tampa Bay area.

Ken is a graduate of the Pennsylvania State University, School of Engineering (1982) and received his Masters degree in Electrical Engineering from the Air Force Institute of Technology in 1983. Ken is a former US Air Force Captain and father of three. He is a member of the National Association of College Admissions Counseling, holds the Certified College Planning Specialist designation and is a CERTIFIED FINANCIAL PLANNER™ professional.

CPSIA information can be obtained at www.ICGtesting.com
Printed in the USA
BVOW071429250112

281341BV00001B/112/P